exploring

STORYBOARDING

exploring

STORYBOARDING

Wendy Tumminello

THOMSON

DELMAR LEARNING™

Australia Canada Mexico Singapore Spain United Kingdom United States

THOMSON

DELMAR LEARNING™

Exploring Storyboarding
Wendy Tumminello

Vice President, Technology and Trades SBU:
Alar Elken

Editorial Director:
Sandy Clark

Senior Acquisitions Editor:
James Gish

Development Editor:
Jaimie Wetzel

Editorial Assistant:
Marissa Maiella

Marketing Director:
Dave Garza

Channel Manager:
William Lawrensen

Marketing Coordinator:
Mark Pierro

Production Director:
Mary Ellen Black

Production Manager:
Larry Main

Production Coordinator:
Dawn Jacobson

Art/Design:
Thomas Stover

Technology Project Manager:
Kevin Smith

Cover Design:
Steven Brower

Cover Image:
J. Allen McFadden

Library of Congress Cataloging-in-Publication Data

Tumminello, Wendy.
  Exploring storyboarding / Wendy Tumminello.—1st ed.
   p. cm.
  Includes bibliographical references and index.
  ISBN 1-4018-2715-2
  1. Storyboards. 2. Commercial art—Vocational guidance— United States. I. Title.
NC1002.S85T86 2004
791.4302'33—dc22
                        2004009136

NOTICE TO THE READER

table of contents

TABLE OF CONTENTS

v

table of contents

TABLE OF CONTENTS

Dom's POV: TRAIN CLOSING, ETC...

| exploring storyboarding |

preface

INTENDED AUDIENCE

A key ingredient to becoming a successful storyboard artist is mastering the visual storytelling process, whether for film, animation, or multimedia. *Exploring Storyboarding* explains the history of storyboards and animatics, and why they are so important to the production process. It also offers to its audience a broad-based understanding of how visual stories are told through technical elements such as composition, lighting, framing, and perspective. Also covered in *Exploring Storyboarding* is a section on the necessary drawing skills required to be a storyboard artist and the materials used.

This book is intended for use by professional schools for film, animation, and game design, as well as for traditional universities that offer production classes. The primary audience for *Exploring Storyboarding* consists of digital media, film, and animation students who must understand how storyboards and animatics contribute to the storytelling process.

Exploring Storyboarding is also useful to professional filmmakers, including directors, producers, and cinematographers, who use storyboards and animatics to communicate their ideas.

BACKGROUND OF THIS TEXT

The evolution of *Exploring Storyboarding* came from my desire to delve more comprehensively into the storyboard process, which plays a pivotal role in visual storytelling. Today with film budgets exceeding $80 million, the need for storyboards has become instrumental for pre-visualizing scenes. Storyboards allow the director or designer to plan on paper the intended message for a project, which saves both time and money during production.

A popular trend amongst directors is to take the pre-visualization process a step further by creating animatics, which are moving storyboards. Animatics are extremely useful for showcasing motion, especially for complex action sequences and special effects.

By creating animatics, directors are able to explore the pacing of shots and how scenes flow together to tell a story. This assists directors in visualizing what scenes will look like before they are actually created.

As you read this book, you will recognize that there are no strict guidelines for creating storyboards or animatics as there are with formatting a screenplay. However, coming to understand the elements of a storyboard, including camera terminology, composition, continuity, lighting, and perspective, are a necessity for any potential storyboard artist.

As you dive into the pages of *Exploring Storyboarding,* don't be afraid to make notes in the margin or try to replicate several of the illustrations. In fact, take it a step further and complete the exercises at the end of each chapter. These specific exercises will guide you in understanding the elements that make up a storyboard.

TEXTBOOK ORGANIZATION

To understand the storyboard process, readers must first become familiar with how stories are structured. In Chapter One, readers explore the hero's journey, elements of a story, and how stories are formatted, which includes the standard screenplay narrative and two-column script. This chapter also defines storyboards, how they are used, and the industries that use them.

Chapter Two provides a brief history of early film and animation in relation to the birth of the modern storyboard at Disney Studios. The chapter also explains the history of aspect ratios, in addition to calculating aspect ratios for television, film, and multimedia storyboards.

Copyright © Cos Russo, Dejavu Worlds

Chapter Three provides an introduction to the visual language of film, animation, and multimedia. Readers will learn specific terminology for a shot, including camera framing, angles, and movement. The chapter also discusses how directional arrows communicate character and camera movement.

Understanding the psychological impact of shots is discussed in Chapter Four. The chapter also addresses the shooting script, shot list, and overhead diagram, along with the storyboard approach for creating thumbnails, roughs, and ultimately the final storyboards.

Chapter Five provides an overview of how the elements of design affect shot arrangement. The chapter also demonstrates how to apply the rule of thirds to storyboard panels, along with how to arrange shots for maximum emotional and psychological impact.

Readers learn how to apply perspective techniques in Chapter Six, to create objects from both high and low angles, along with how camera lenses affect depth of field.

Chapter Seven explores how light can dramatically affect a composition. The chapter explores three-point lighting and the direction of light, along with the differences between high-key and low-key lighting.

Chapter Eight looks at the importance of continuity and how it contributes to visually telling a story. This chapter explains the significance of the line of action, along with what it means to cross the line. Included in this chapter are explanations of screen direction, match on action, cut-ins, and cut-aways.

Chapters Nine through Eleven look specifically at industries that use storyboards, including Advertising, Animation, Multimedia, and Film. In Chapter Nine readers explore the process for creating storyboards for both feature and television animation, along with the nuances of creating storyboards for live-action film. Chapter Ten describes the process for creating an advertising campaign, along with the key people involved. The chapter also demonstrates what elements are needed to create a presentation storyboard. In Chapter Eleven readers explore storyboarding for multimedia CD-ROMs and Web sites to video games. This chapter identifies the key elements of the game design, including the script, game play, and the creation of flowcharts and storyboards.

Chapter Twelve explores the nature of animatics and its usage at both animation and film studios. This chapter explores the different types of animatics, the importance of pacing, and preparing the storyboard for inclusion in the animatic.

Chapter Thirteen illustrates drawing techniques for storyboarding, which includes quick sketches, perspective drawing, and drawing the human figure in motion.

Chapter Fourteen addresses career opportunities for the storyboard artist. This chapter reviews required skills for the artist, interview techniques, and criteria needed to create online and flat-art portfolios.

FEATURES

The following list provides some of the salient features of the text:

- Objectives clearly state the learning goals of each chapter.
- Profiles of successful storyboard artists are included, along with their important industry advice and inspiration.
- Review questions and exercises reinforce material presented in the each chapter.
- Storyboard examples from major motion films.
- Reviews and explains the storytelling process.
- Examines the elements of composition, including balance, contrast and similarity, and open and closed framing.
- Demonstrates the process for creating storyboards from thumbnails to roughs to final storyboards.
- Explores the importance of animatics in the studio and usage during on-site shoots.

about the author

ABOUT THE AUTHOR

Wendy Tumminello is an award-winning multimedia producer and designer. She is currently a faculty member for the Digital Media Production Department of the Art Institute of Washington.

As a Producer/Designer for CapDisc (a division of Philips Media), Wendy designed and produced numerous multimedia projects for both education and entertainment. Her work culminated in being named one of the Top 100 Producers by *AV Video and Multimedia Producer Magazine*. Over the years, Wendy has produced and directed several video projects, along with the recently completed documentary *Hitting the Right Chord*, for which she received numerous grants to make a reality.

Wendy has spoken at several conferences on the topic of independent filmmaking, and has enjoyed the success of having her work shown both domestically and internationally at various film festivals. She holds a B.S. in Marketing from the University of Maryland, and an M.F.A. in Visual Media from American University. Wendy is currently a member of Women in Film, The International Documentary Association, and The University Film and Video Association.

HOW TO USE
THIS TEXT

The following features can be found throughout this book:

▶ ## Objectives

Learning objectives start off each chapter. They describe the competencies the readers should achieve upon understanding the chapter material.

▶ ## Tips and Quotes

Tips provide special hints, practical techniques, and information to the reader. Quotes from professionals also provide industry advice and inspiration.

Sidebars

Sidebars appear throughout the text, offering additional valuable information on specific topics.

Review Questions and Exercises

Review questions and exercises are located at the end of each chapter and allow the reader to assess their understanding of the chapter. Exercises are intended to reinforce chapter material through practical application.

The Storyboard Artist at Work

These career profiles are interspersed throughout the text. Each features a successful storyboard artist in the field.

E.RESOURCE

This electronic manual was developed to assist instructors in planning and implementing their instructional programs. It includes sample syllabi for using this book in either an 11- or 15-week course. It provides answers to the review questions found in the text, tips for assessing completed exercises assigned in the book, and a list of additional resources. It also includes PowerPoint lecture slides that highlight main topics and provide a framework for discussion.

ISBN: 1401827462

ACKNOWLEDGMENTS

My many thanks go out to Jim Gish for his support and enthusiasm for this project along with the entire Delmar team. My appreciation goes out to each and every one of you: Marissa Maiella, Tom Stover, Rachel Baker, and Dawn Jacobson.

My appreciation to Allen McFadden for the cover art and numerous illustrations you created for this book, along with David Phillips, Jamie McCullough, Gerardo Ramirez, Luis Alfaro, and Dorian Soto for your contributions. I'd also like to extend my gratitude to Brain Immel for your involvement in helping me write the Animatics chapter, and to Matt Karol, Warren Drummond, Don Anderson, Bo Hampton, Murray Taylor, and Cos Russo for taking the time out of your busy schedules to speak with me about your careers. A big thank you to my students, and the many talented artists whose illustrations appear throughout this book.

I'd like to thank Suzy Garber for not only reading my chapters, but also for supporting and encouraging me to do my best. To my friend and mentor, Jean-Christophe Hyacinthe for your contributions to this book. And to my family for always supporting me.

A very special thank you to Jaimie Wetzel. Your patience was more than appreciated and your enthusiasm steadfast. I could not have done it without your support.

Delmar Learning and the author would also like to thank the following reviewers for their valuable suggestions and expertise:

BRIAN ARNOLD
Media Arts & Animation Department
Art Institutes International Minnesota
Minneapolis, Minnesota

ERIC ELDER
Media Arts & Animation Department
Art Institute of California – Santa Monica
Santa Monica, California

ERIC ENGBERG
Digital Video and Media Production Department
Minnesota School of Business
Brooklyn Center, Minnesota

LARRY MIGLIORI and **ALEX PIEJKO**
Art Department
Mohawk Valley Community College
Utica, New York

RICHARD PALATINI
Senior V.P./ Associate Creative Director
Gianettino & Meredith Advertising
Short Hills, New Jersey

DAVID RUDE
Dunwoody School of Technology
Saint Paul, Minnesota

MICHAEL TRACY
Media Arts & Animation Department
Art Institute of California – Orange County
Santa Ana, California

Wendy Tumminello
2004

QUESTIONS AND FEEDBACK

Delmar Learning and the authors welcome your questions and feedback. If you have suggestions that you think others would benefit from, please let us know and we will try to include them in the next edition.

To send us your questions and/or feedback, you can contact the publisher at:

Delmar Learning
Executive Woods
5 Maxwell Drive
Clifton Park, NY 12065
Attn: Graphic Arts Team
800-998-7498

Or the author at:
The Art Institute — Washington DC
1820 N. Fort Myer Drive
Arlington, VA 22209
tuminw@hotmail.com

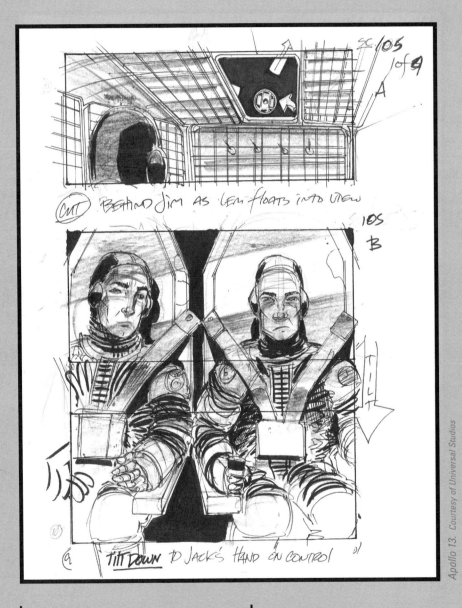

| visual storytelling and storyboards |

objectives

introduction

We are constantly confronted with visuals in our daily lives, from the most obvious (television, movies, the Internet) to books, magazines, newspapers, and comics. They are found in our living rooms, schools, public transportation systems, our dreams, and even in our skies.

Each visual tells us a story, whether it is a message to buy something or to entertain us. Visuals can make us feel happy, agitated, skeptical, and influence our decisions. For example, an image of pearly white teeth in an advertisement may lead us to buy a new brand of toothpaste, or a child playing in a sandbox may bring a smile to our face.

The storyboard is the visual version of the script. It consists of a number of panels that show the visual action of a sequence in a logical narrative. But whereas stories entertain, the storyboard is used as a tool for production or to assist in the selling of ideas to clients. The next several pages will provide an overview of the scripting process and the use of storyboards within different industries.

VISUAL STORYTELLING

Storyboarding the visual flow of a narrative is a relatively new concept, but visual storytelling is not. In fact, telling visual stories has been around for thousands of years. Early rock paintings were used as a form of communication before speech was even developed. It is believed that these visual paintings told stories about friends, animal attacks, how they hunted, and so forth.

Over the last century, visual storytelling has been taken to new heights with the emergence of photography, television, film, and computers. Graphic illustrations such as photographs, comics, and magazines communicate their message without motion. Figure 1-1 of a pool shark leaning against a pool table raises several questions. Who is the man? Where is he playing pool? Who is he playing against? Is he playing for money? The image conveys the intended message through staging the character and props, establishing the background, and portraying the action.

figure **1-1**

Visual storytelling.
© Jean-Christophe Hyacinthe

Movies and animation are linear forms of visual storytelling where the audience listens and watches passively. Games and multimedia applications, on the other hand, are interactive programs where the user both actively views and manipulates the program. A user of a game doesn't just sit back with a bucket of popcorn and watch the story unfold, but interacts with the message whether it's plotting a murder, looking for clues, or dodging a hailstorm of punches from an opponent.

figure |1-2|

Shrike storyboard.

© Bo Hampton

Although the means and the methods of storytelling may have changed over time, the storyteller's purpose has pretty much stayed the same—to communicate a message to an audience. A storyteller's effectiveness is based on drawing an audience into the story and capturing their attention. This is often accomplished by the message that the story and the visuals deliver.

VISUALS VERSUS THE STORY

Show me. Don't tell me. This is a phrase I often communicate to my students. It also happens to be the basis of writing visual content. If you *tell* a story, you try to entice the audience into imagining its content. However, if you are going to *show* the audience, you must rely less on telling and more on showing. Think of it this way: when you *show* a story, you are molding the message into visual imagery. Let's look at an example of telling versus showing.

Telling Example

Jake, who was considered the bully of the neighborhood, stood on the corner of Tenth and Main in his blue jeans, black T-shirt, and a cigarette pack rolled up in his sleeve. The rest of the kids avoided the corner where Jake stood. They were intimidated by the high school dropout who derived pleasure from flicking the burning embers of his cigarette into the hair of any kid who crossed his path.

The above example *tells* the viewer what Jake's demeanor and personality is like. It is up to the audience to imagine the expression and actions of both Jake and the children.

Showing Example

Jake, a burly teen with pock marks on his cheeks and skull tattoo scrawled across his bicep, kicks a scuffed military boot in the dirt. The dust circles his feet as he pulls a cigarette from behind his ear and slips it between his lips. His eyes dart to several school children scurrying single file down a dirt path. He settles his gaze on a pint-sized boy with a Space Rangers backpack slung over his small shoulders. Jake smirks as he takes a long drag from his cigarette and quickly steps forward toward the boy.

Now that's more like it. The audience is able to *see* Jake kick the dirt up as he pulls a cigarette from behind his ear. When writing visual content, you want to *show* the actions of the characters, the aesthetics of locations, and how the characters feel.

ELEMENTS OF A STORY

Most stories start out as an idea without structure. For instance, think about your dreams. Usually they are nothing more than fragments of images strung together. This is how ideas usually germinate. They often begin as abstract images that take form over time, as structure and order are later added to the mix. Let's take a look at a very simple example. There are three images: *bridge, boat* and *bicyclist.* Alone they are no more than words without meaning or interest to an audience. But what if you gave those words meaning through structure. Stories need to be about something. Therefore, we could take our *bicyclist* and put him in a situation where he had to get across the *bridge* to deliver a package within the hour. We are now beginning to structure our story with an action or goal on the part of the bicyclist. But wait. All good stories need conflict. What if the *bridge* goes up to let a *boat* pass, making it difficult for the bicyclist, to reach his goal in time? Using a time element, or *ticking clock,* raises the stakes for our *bicyclist,* as in figure 1-3.

Questions that the story raises are: Will the bicyclist make it in time? What will happen if he doesn't? The author must have these questions answered by the end of the story if the audience is to walk away satisfied. Once the problem is solved—and the package is delivered in time (or not)—the story is resolved.

Dramatic structure is usually defined as the beginning, middle, and end, or if it is a screenplay, act one, act two, and act three. No matter what you call it, the purpose is the same, which is to structure the flow of a story to give it meaning.

figure **1-3**

Elements of a story.
Courtesy of J. Allen McFadden

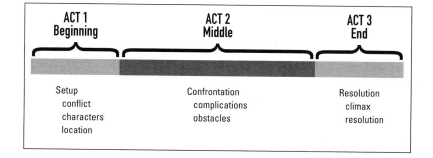

figure **1-4**

Three-act story structure.

The Hero's Journey

In a galaxy far, far away, Luke Skywalker began a journey that took him from his home to new worlds in which he encountered both charming and peculiar characters. We have heard similar stories, from recent motion pictures to great works of literature.

The hero must take many steps to fulfill her journey. These steps begin with describing the hero's ordinary world to the point where the hero takes on the problem and enters the extraordinary world. This is the beginning of the story, or act one. As a story unravels, there are many obstacles and complications that the hero must face. During this part of the journey, the hero comes across both foes and friends alike, which is the middle of the story, or act two. Finally, the hero reaches the point where all seems lost, before the final climax and resolution.

figure 1-5

The basic elements of the hero's journey.

The Hero's Journey

The hero's journey can be traced back to Greek mythology and great works of literature. The hero's journey is still followed today from major motion films to games and animation. The following is the basic steps included in the hero's journey.

The Calling:

Sometimes the calling is a traumatic event. This may include having something taken away and the quest by the hero to regain it. The calling, however, doesn't always have to be agonizing, but instead may creep up on the hero. This may include discontentment with the way the hero lives her life, and the quest to find what is missing.

Threshold

The threshold is the point where the hero takes action, or passes from the ordinary world into the extraordinary world, which is filled with danger and challenges. It is at this stage that the hero will meet people who may block her path. The hero may also meet a mentor at this stage, or helpers, that provide stability to the hero.

Initiation

It is during this stage that the hero faces both challenges and obstacles on her journey. In the beginning of the journey the challenges may seem relatively easy, but as the story progresses, the hero will face much more difficult tasks, which forces the hero to change and grow. It is also at this stage that the hero may meet foes that are disguised as friends. It is up to the hero to use her judgment to recognize friend from foe.

The Abyss

This is the point where the hero must face her greatest fears. Sometimes the challenges become too great. It is here that the hero must either surrender to the fear or retreat.

Transformation

When the hero conquers the abyss, transformation occurs. Part of this process includes revelation, or a dramatic change in the way the hero views life.

The Return

The return is the final stage of the journey. This is the point where the hero returns to her ordinary life, but not without growing as a person. The hero may become stronger, wiser, or may become enlightened.

Understanding how stories are put together, which includes the hero's journey, is an integral part to creating storyboards. Let's take a brief look at each phase of the visual storytelling process from beginning, to middle, to end.

The Beginning

The beginning, or act one, in film, television, and animation, is where the storyteller sets up the characters, location, and conflict of the story. Several questions that need to be answered include: Who are the characters? Where are they? When does the story take place (the future, past, or present)? Why are the characters there?

Dynamic stories may begin with a hook that grabs the audience's attention, such as a murder or kidnapping. Action sequences make great hooks, although they are not the only types of scenes that keep the audience watching. For example, the hook in a story may be a couple breaking up or it may be as simple as a character receiving an eviction notice. The hook should leave the audience asking questions. For instance, why did the woman get evicted from her apartment? Who kidnapped the girl? What caused the couple to split apart? If the audience is hooked, they will undoubtedly want to know what happens next and keep watching.

figure | 1-6 |

Storyboard panel from the film *AKA*.
© *Invision Films*
Artist: Adrian Bryant

Visuals are extremely important to hook the audience and to set up the hero's journey. In the movie *Fight Club*, the first image we see of Jack, the film's protagonist, is with a gun barrel in his mouth before a struggle ensues. As we watch the film, we want to know who Jack is, and how he got himself into such a predicament.

The beginning also defines the hero's goal. Is it to save the kidnapped princess, get a job, save the world, or defeat the town's evil mayor? In the animated film *Chicken Run*, the protagonist's goal is one of survival and to escape the chicken coup, which resembles a Nazi occupation camp. In the video game *Sim City 2000*, the goal of the player is to build and manage a city. In *Legally Blonde 2*, Elle Wood's goal is to get an anti-animal testing bill passed in Washington DC, a city notorious for behind your back deals and disillusionment.

The Middle

The middle, or act two, is where the hero faces many complications and obstacles in his search to reach the goal or solve a problem. The middle contains many twists and turns, and keeps raising the stakes to keep the story interesting and the tension building. In *Gladiator*, for example, we witness Maximus go from General to slave. His family murdered, Maximus loses both his position and his name as he battles many opponents in the Gladiator ring. The stakes for Maximus become even higher as he is forced to reveal his identity to Commodus, the evil ruler of Rome, who wants nothing more than to see him dead.

The hero often faces a turning point in act two, which takes the story in a different direction. In an episode of *The Simpsons*, Homer's mission changes from trying to find a job to lobbying for a stop sign at a dangerous intersection.

By the end of act two, all seems lost for the hero. In *Legally Blonde*, Elle quits law school and her job as an intern on a murder trial, because she cannot seem to escape the "dumb blonde" stereotype. In *Gladiator*, Maximus's faithful servant is murdered, and Commodus imprisons Maximus.

The End

The end, or act three, is where the climax and resolution of the problem occurs: the hero's goal is attained, the problem is solved, etc. Many endings include a showdown, or final confrontation, which is often between the protagonist and antagonist. The action becomes most intense near the end as the hero makes a last stand. This is where the guy gets the girl, the soldier saves the princess, the good guy captures the thief, or the slave defeats the enemy before ultimately succumbing to his wounds.

Great endings sometimes include a *ticking clock*, which is the race against time in order to reach the goal. A classic ending is three seconds on the clock with one down left as the football team makes the winning touchdown.

| TIP |

As a guideline when writing a screenplay, act two should be twice as long as act one.

One screenplay page is equivalent to one minute of screen time.

WHY FORMAT THE STORY?

The script is the blueprint for a production. It provides the writer with a means of communication that is intended for the project's director and crewmembers. It is the screenwriter's job to tell the story, not plan the shots. This is the director's job.

Formatting a screenplay helps with the rhythm of a story through the choice of camera positions, narration, dialogue, and the juxtaposition of scenes. The format guides the producer or director with visualizing the writer's concepts and ideas. The script is also formatted because it is much easier for the director of a production to have it broken down into numbered scenes, schedules, and prop lists. In most situations, the script will be formatted in either a standard screenplay format or as a two-column script.

Standard Screenplay Format

Screenplays are not intended for audiences to read as they would a novel. Rather, they are used as a production tool for the director and crewmembers in the development of a film, game, or animation. The screenplay has become the Hollywood standard, which includes several elements such as the slug line, scene description, and dialogue.

Slug Lines

Each new scene needs slug lines—scene headings that describe the location of a scene, the time of the scene, and whether it takes place inside (interior) or outside (exterior). Slug lines should be short and to the point, such as:

- EXT. BASKETBALL COURT—DAY
- INT. AIRPORT TERMINAL— NIGHT

```
INT. POLICE AREA — NIGHT

A sea of BLUE UNIFORMS swamp metal desks. The EXPLOSION of
typewriters fire off from several areas as suspects are
being questioned.

Detective Frank makes his way to a utilitarian desk piled
high with police reports. He pulls up two metal chairs and
motions for the girls to sit down. Detective Frank pushes
aside a box of chocolate donuts and coffee mug. He sits on
the edge of the desk close to the girls.

                    FRANK
          Sergeant Roscoe tells me you two
          have a murder to report.

                    LILY
          We're not exactly sure if
          he's dead.

                    FRANK
          And who is this possible dead
          person?

                    LILY
          The Mayor.

                    FRANK
          Mayor Beasley?

                    LILY
          That's the one.

                    FRANK
          Why do you think the Mayor's dead?
          Did you see something?

                    LILY
          Well, not exactly.

                    FRANK
          How then?


Lily scowls at Jessie whose gaze is transfixed on the box
of donuts. Lily looks back at Detective Frank.

                    LILY
          I dreamt it.
```

figure | 1-7 |

Standard screenplay format.

Description

The description within a screenplay includes where the action takes place and the elements of a scene, such as the characters and objects. When writing a story, it is sometimes better to show the audience than reveal information through dialogue. The description should communicate images that disclose details the audience needs to see. For example, images of a mother absently touching frayed toys in a child's room is much richer than explaining that the child no longer lives at home.

Dialogue

An important rule is to *show* it rather than *say* it. However, that does not mean there is no reason for dialogue. On the contrary. You should use dialogue when you want to express a character's emotions, explore the interactions between characters and the environment, and to move the story forward.

Two-Column Script

The two-column script is frequently used for corporate videos, documentaries, multimedia, and news. The script is broken into two columns—for video and audio. The left column contains video information, with audio on the right. Every visual and audio element is specified in the appropriate column. For example, information about camera framing and movement is usually described in the video column, and information about dialogue and music in the audio column.

Many video and news people use the two-column script format because the visuals are easily synchronized to the audio.

EXAMPLE TWO-COLUMN SCRIPT FORMAT

Partial Cereal Script
: 30 sec.

VIDEO	AUDIO
MS of boy eating cereal at kitchen table	MUSIC FADES UP AND UNDER
TWO SHOT of brother licking his lips	
Cut to CU of brother's face	BROTHER: Can I have some?
Cut to MS of boy merrily eating a heaping spoonful of cereal	
Cut to two shot of brothers at table. Brother pulls out a miniature toy car, jacks, and bubble gum	BROTHER: I'll trade you my jeep, three jacks and a piece of bubble gum?
Cut to ECU of boy's eyes shifting down at toys then back up. Pull out to the two brothers.	BOY: Nope.

figure | 1-8

Two-column script format.

STORYBOARDS

Storyboards are a series of sketches that are used as a planning tool to visually show how the action of a story unfolds. The closest visual relation to the storyboard is the comic strip minus the dialogue balloons. But whereas comic strips entertain, the storyboard is a tool that facilitates production.

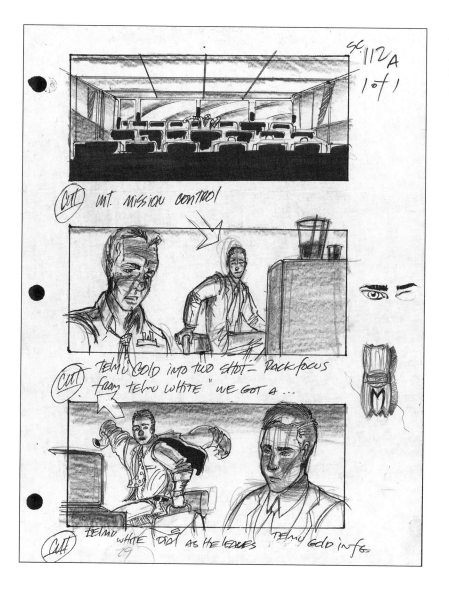

figure | 1-9 |

Storyboard from the film *Apollo 13*.
Courtesy of Universal Studios

The main purpose of the storyboard is to clearly convey the narrative flow of a story by defining the challenges and problems of a project. Therefore, understanding the elements of the storytelling process is of utmost importance for the storyboard artist to do her job.

Storyboards also assist in the timing of a sequence, experimenting with camera angles, movement, and continuity amongst the elements within the frame.

Storyboards are revised and adjusted to accommodate the industry for which they are being used. The most commonly used are the production storyboard and the presentation storyboard.

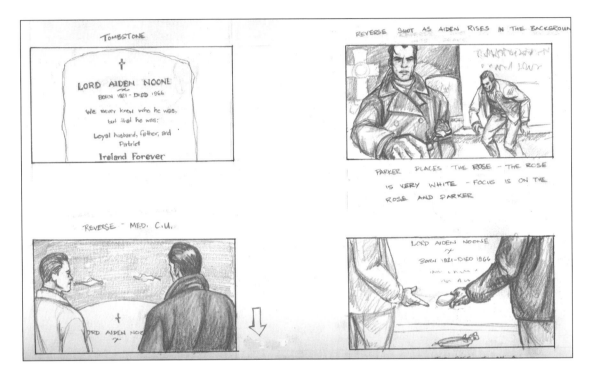

The production storyboard is also referred to as the shooting board or editorial storyboard. It is used to assist crewmembers during production for framing, blocking, and composing a shot. A presentation storyboard, on the other hand, is used to sell ideas to clients or to evaluate existing campaigns. Both types of storyboards are discussed at length in later chapters.

WHO USES STORYBOARDS?

Storyboard use may vary within each industry, but the purpose is the same and that is to visually communicate project ideas and objectives. Storyboards are incorporated into many industries including industrial, advertising, and interactive design. The following is a partial list of the different uses for storyboards; several will be discussed in depth in later chapters.

Advertising Campaigns

Advertising agencies use presentation storyboards to sell campaign strategies to clients or for use in focus groups. Storyboards that reflect campaign ideas are highly detailed and include key frames only.

Video Games

Video games take a lot of preplanning, including brainstorming the game concepts and user interaction. Once the story lines are developed, the game designer creates the storyboards for each scene of the game, including the cinematic, or full-motion video sequences, that introduce a story and act as the user's reward for excelling in game play.

Television Series

Usually when working in television, the director will storyboard only complex sequences. Some television shows that use storyboards include *CSI, The West Wing, ER, Babylon 5,* and *Witchblade.*

Multimedia

CD-ROMs for education, training, or "how-to" programs can be extremely complex, requiring extensive interactivity. Storyboards usually contain a sketch of each screen, along with notes about the content of particular images, the function of specific buttons, and how video and sound is to be presented.

Web Design

Storyboards are useful to the development team for Web design, in defining and grouping elements such as graphics, animation, video, and illustrations. Storyboards assist the team in understanding the structure of a site, and how that information is presented.

Industrial and Governmental Videos

Storyboards are an indispensable tool for presenting ideas to clients when creating industrial and/or governmental videos. Storyboards promote effective decision-making, and help to set strategies, and solve problems.

CHAPTER SUMMARY

Visual storytelling has been taken to new heights with the emergence of television, film, computers, and animation. Most stories begin in our imagination and are then given structure. Stories with structure have a beginning, middle, and end that explore the hero's journey. The journey begins with the hook, which grabs the viewer's attention. However, every good story needs conflict. If there is no conflict, there is no story. Formatting a script is very important, as it helps organize the story elements for both the director and the producer of a production.

Storyboards are sketches that are used to visually show how a story unfolds. The storyboard is similar to the comic strip, but rather than entertain, it is used as a planning tool to visualize the director's ideas. Storyboards are used in various industries, including advertising, film, Web design, and multimedia.

in review

1. What is visual storytelling?

2. How does visual storytelling differ from film and animation to interactive games?

3. What are two ways to format a story?

4. What is the difference between showing and telling?

5. What are elements of the hero's journey?

6. What is the hook of a story?

7. What is a slug line?

8. What are storyboards? How are they similar to the comic strip?

9. What industries use storyboards?

exercises

1. Write a short scene that illustrates the principles of showing versus telling.

2. Research companies that use storyboard artists. What type of storyboards do these companies create? What is the role of the storyboard artist in these fields?

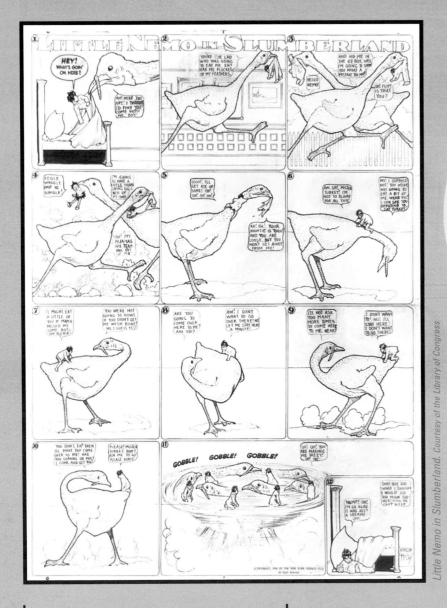

origins of storyboards and aspect ratios

objectives

Learn the early history of the storyboard

Understand where storyboards fit in the visual storytelling process

Learn the history of aspect ratios

Understand the difference between pan & scan and letterboxing

Demonstrate how to calculate aspect ratios

introduction

Visual storytelling has been around for thousands of years, but the technique of storyboarding is a relatively new concept. Disney Studios first conceived of storyboards with the rise of the animated short in the early 1930s. Soon thereafter, film directors were planning complex sequences by sketching how they envisioned particular scenes to unfold. Directors also relied on storyboard panels that were the same size, or aspect ratio, of the movie screen. Aspect ratios changed over the years as new technologies, such as television, were introduced.

This chapter provides insight into the origins of the storyboard. It also provides details of the historical significance of aspect ratios and why they are important to the process of sketching storyboards.

ORIGINS OF STORYBOARDS AND ASPECT RATIOS

EARLY HISTORY OF THE STORYBOARD

The birth of the cinematic image was a spectacle as audiences watched the first pictures flicker across the screen. The Lumière brothers were credited with the first cinematic screening in 1895 of workers at the Lumière factory strolling through the front gate. Audiences were awed as they watched everyday events, such as a train pulling into a station and a baby eating. Although the public was fascinated, the Lumières considered their many recordings as a purely scientific method to record reality, and saw no real future for this new innovation.

In stark contrast to the Lumières was George Méliès, who was a magician by trade. Méliès used the camera not to record everyday occurrences, but to document his magic tricks. He created stylized sets for his elaborate film narratives. His best-known work is the 1902 film *A Trip to the Moon,* which is a tale of space explorers who land on the moon.

figure |2-1|

A Trip to the Moon.

With the evolution of film came more elaborate stories and sophisticated camera techniques. Although the modern storyboard was still years away during cinema's early history, directors such as Sergi Eisenstein and Cecil B. DeMille relied on artist sketches to help develop story ideas. Eisenstein created a multitude of his own sketches before undertaking the 1925 film *The Battleship Potemkin* and later the 1931 film *Black Majesty*. These sketches guided him for how the action should move within each scene. Cecil B. DeMille, the famed Hollywood director, used the talents of artist Dan Sayre Groesbeck to assist him in visualizing the dramatic scenes for his 1923 film *The Ten Commandments*.

Real strides toward the birth of the modern storyboard took place not in film, but in animation. During animation's infancy, studios relied solely on their artists to generate story ideas. Animators were responsible for cartoons, which were often no more than simple gags and jokes strung together around a theme. Early animations such as *Krazy Kat* and *Bobby Bumps* were five-minute cartoons with no story line. This was how Winsor McCay, who is considered the father of animation, got his start. McCay's first animation was based on his popular newspaper strip *Little Nemo in Slumberland*. It was not until cartoonist Ed McManus wagered McCay that he could not "bring a dinosaur to life" that the public became aware of this new technology. As a result of the bet, McCay created a series of drawings for his 1914 animation *Gertie the Dinosaur*. McCay animated *Gertie* almost single-handedly, creating over 10,000 sketches, which he then hand-colored frame by frame. *Gertie*, like so many animations to follow, was an experiment in motion rather than a fully formed story with a beginning, middle, and end.

figure | 2-2 |

Gertie the Dinosaur.
Courtesy of the Library of Congress

Arguably, the most successful and influential of these early animators were Max and Dave Fleischer, creators of the *Koko the Clown* and *Betty Boop* cartoons. In the 1920s and early 1930s, Fleischer Studios had no story department and often relied on their animators to generate stories based on gags. The Fleischers gave the animators ideas for scenes, but nothing was ever written down on paper. There was no script. Rather, Dave Fleischer would make the rounds every morning among the animators and suggest where more gags should be added.

figure | 2-3 |

Koko the Clown.
Courtesy of the Library of Congress

In the beginning of his career, Walt Disney imitated the style of Fleischer and McCay with his animated short *Alice in Cartoonland*. But as his interest in live-action films peaked, so did his motivation to think beyond the scope of presenting cartoons as a series of uncomplicated sight gags. Disney and his small crew started sketching out ideas for stories after studying the films of Charlie Chaplin and Buster Keaton. They studied camera angles, camera movement, and timing. Over time, their hard work paid off. In 1928 Disney released *Plane Crazy*, the first Mickey Mouse cartoon. *Plane Crazy* was meticulously crafted from story sketches that looked similar to a comic strip. The story sketches included dynamic camera angles, framing, and character action. Accompanying the sketches were action descriptions for each scene, written out on a separate piece of paper.

Disney animators worked as both gagmen and animators, but as they experimented with story sketches, Walt realized the need for a separate story department with its own writers. Ted Sears, who began his career as a gagman for Disney, was appointed to head up this newly formed department in the early 1930s. From this point forward, animators were no longer responsible for both the story and the art. Instead, they worked with writers, who developed the story ideas.

Before too long, the number of sketches that each project generated grew to the extent that understanding a story's logical flow and content became an increasingly difficult task. Story man Webb Smith had a solution: he pinned all the sketches and dialogue to the wall in a sequence from beginning to end. Smith then reworked the sequence of shots until he felt that story continuity was achieved. The first cartoon recognized for using Smith's method of storyboarding was the 1933 cartoon *The Three Little Pigs*.

Early Disney storyboards were a collaborative process between the writer and animator, making it easy to visualize ideas by shifting scenes, and adding and deleting drawings. Over time, the process was streamlined so that eventually all ideas submitted for review to Walt Disney were on storyboards. If approved by Disney, the boards were used to coordinate production. One of the earliest and most well-known uses of the modern storyboard was for the animated feature film *Snow White and the Seven Dwarves*. Storyboards played an integral role in the development of *Snow White,* with thousands of sketches being generated to bring the story to life. Disney had the storyboard panels pinned to a wall, then he acted out the scenes of the movie to the crew working on the production.

As storyboard usage became more common, and animation studios flourished, live-action directors took notice. Film directors began to preplan their films, storyboarding elaborate action sequences and special effects. For *Citizen Kane*, Orson Welles storyboarded complex lighting sequences and scenes that used "deep-focus" cinematography. Producer David O. Selznick, whose films include *Gone with the Wind* and *Duel in the Sun,* worked with illustrator William Cameron Menzies, who storyboarded many early films. Menzies was credited with the visual design of *Gone with the Wind,* in which he created hundreds of drawings that encompassed framing, composition, and camera movement.

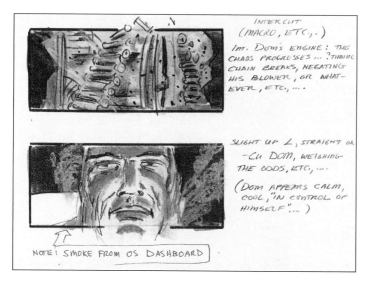

INTER CUT
(MACRO, ETC,.)

Int. Dom's ENGINE: THE
CHAOS PROGRESSES ... ?TIMING
CHAIN BREAKS, NEGATING
HIS BLOWER, OR WHAT-
EVER, ETC, ...

SLIGHT UP L, STRAIGHT ON
- CU DOM, WEIGHING
THE ODDS, ETC, ...

(DOM APPEARS CALM,
COOL, "IN CONTROL OF
HIMSELF",...)

NOTE! SMOKE FROM OS DASHBOARD

figure 2-4

Storyboard from
2 Fast 2 Furious.
Courtesy of Universal Studios.

Alfred Hitchcock, the director of such films as *Vertigo, Rear Window,* and *Psycho,* considered his films as storyboards come to life. Hitchcock drew many of his own storyboards, as well as enlisted the help of the famous title designer Saul Bass, who storyboarded the intricate shower sequence in *Psycho,* which included over seventy-five camera setups. Hitchcock referred to Bass's storyboards as a guideline for setting up the murder. The shower sequence was not only powerful for audiences, but also for other directors who mimicked Hitchcock's style. Martin Scorcese was one such director who studied the shower sequence of fast cuts and dramatic camera angles, to model the storyboard for the LaMotta/Robinson fight sequence in *Raging Bull.*

From the 1930s through the 1970s, many live-action directors only storyboarded special effects and complex action sequences. This was the case with the many James Bond films that were created during the 1960s and 1970s. Artist Syd Cain choreographed the storyboards for the key action sequences for the film *From Russia*

figure 2-5

Alfred Hitchcock.
Courtesy of the Library of Congress

With Love. He later went on to create both concept art and storyboards for such Bond films as *Live and Let Die*, *On Her Majesty's Secret Service*, and *GoldenEye*. On the film *Live and Let Die*, Cain created detailed storyboards for three intricate action sequences that had never been tried before. Storyboarding such scenes allowed the director to visualize on paper what would work without going through the expense of having to shoot different variations of the scene.

As films became more expensive to create, many directors took note of the efficiency that storyboards provided. The storyboard process became particularly important to directors who had several units involved in shooting different scenes. For big budget films, such as *Raiders of the Lost Ark*, the creation of storyboards ensured that all units involved in staging scenes were on the same page.

Today many directors storyboard the entire production for a film or animation. Directors such as Terry Gilliam, John Lasseter, M. Night Shyamalan, Ron Howard, John Singleton, Ridley Scott, the Coen brothers, Martin Scorsese, and Brian De Palma all use storyboards to visualize their ideas.

WHAT ARE ASPECT RATIOS?

Have you ever watched a film on television and, just before the movie starts, the words "This film has been modified from its original format" appear. If you're like many people, you probably thought "what original format?" This format refers to the shape of the screen, or size relationship between its width and height. Since there are many different aspect ratios in use for film, the image has to be modified to fit the television screen.

The first number in an aspect ratio indicates the frame's width, relative to its height. For example, 1.5:1 is an aspect ratio. The first number, 1.5, represents the width of the frame, whereas the second number, 1, stands for the height. The 1.5:1 ratio tells us that for every one unit of height, there are 1.5 units of width.

figure 2-6

Aspect ratio formula.

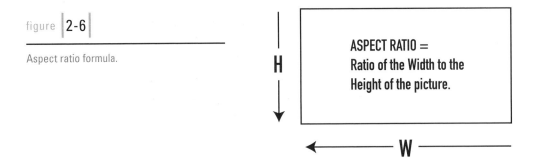

ASPECT RATIO =
Ratio of the Width to the
Height of the picture.

HISTORY OF ASPECT RATIOS

In the early days of film production, movies were created using an aspect ratio of 1.33:1, which is the ratio for 35 mm film. When sound was incorporated into motion pictures, the aspect ratio was adjusted to 1.37:1 to make room for an optical soundtrack on the film frame. This new ratio became known throughout the industry as the Academy Ratio. Films produced in a 1.37:1 aspect ratio include *The Wizard of Oz, Gone with the Wind, Citizen Kane,* and *Casablanca.* When these films are shown today, there is no need for additional formatting to play on a standard television set.

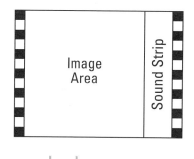

figure | **2-7**

1.37:1 film frame with optical soundtrack.

At the height of film popularity in the early 1930s, an estimated 95 million people attended the theater. Families would frequent the movies three or four times a week, and kids would go every Saturday morning. That all changed when television was introduced, which adopted the same 1.33:1 aspect ratio of the film industry. By the mid-1950s, the number of people attending the movies decreased to 45 million. Movie attendance dropped further to 20 million in the late 1960s, as television penetrated over 90 percent of homes. By 1970, Hollywood needed to provide audiences with an entertainment experience they could not get at home. What they gave them was wider screen movies, which translated into a bigger left to right dimension than the square shape of a television screen. A wider image fills more of our peripheral vision and, as a result, is more intense and realistic because the effect imitates the way we actually see the world. Studios began to compose their films in various widescreen ratios including Cinerama, CinemaScope, and Panavision.

Cinerama

The movie industry was in a quandary after television adopted the same aspect ratio. One of the ways that the film industry fought back was with the introduction of Cinerama, with an aspect ratio of 2.60:1. The widescreen technique was introduced in New York in the 1952 show entitled *This is Cinerama.* The Cinerama experience was a three-camera, three-projector setup that transmitted the film image onto a curved screen.

figure | 2-8a |

Cinerama screen.
Courtesy of the American
WideScreen Museum

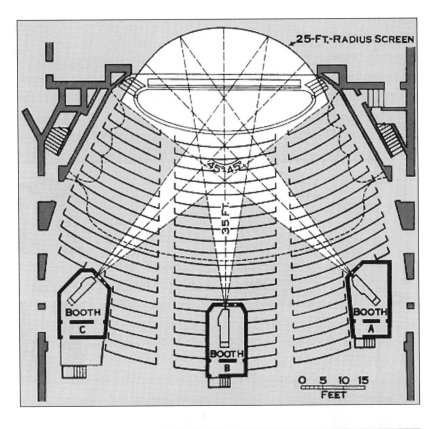

figure | 2-8b |

An example of Cinerama.
Courtesy of the American
WideScreen Museum

The first Cinerama images were of a roller coaster ride. The viewers felt as if they were in the first car as it sped up, down, and around the tracks. There were seven movies released under the Cinerama moniker, including *How the West Was Won, South Seas Adventure,* and *Seven Wonders of the World.* Cinerama ultimately was abandoned because of the high cost of outfitting theaters with multiple cameras and projectors.

CinemaScope

Twentieth Century Fox introduced CinemaScope one year after Cinerama made its entrance as the widescreen experience. The CinemaScope process required outfitting cameras with an anamorphic lens, which photographs the film image and then compresses it. When the image is ready to be screened, another anamorphic lens is used to uncompress the footage. When first introduced, the aspect ratio for CinemaScope was 2.66:1, but ultimately was reduced to 2.55:1. Films produced in CinemaScope include Disney's *20,000 Leagues Under the Sea, Lady and the Tramp, In Like Flint,* and *Rope.* This process lasted until the late 1960s.

figure | 2-9 |

CinemaScope screen.
Courtesy of the American WideScreen Museum

Panavision

Panavision followed on the heels of CinemaScope by creating anamorphic lenses in the late 1950s. Panavision reduced some of the issues that CinemaScope was having with compression, which ultimately led to it becoming the standard choice within the industry. The aspect ratios for Panavision are 2.35:1 and 1.85:1, which are the current film standards.

COMMON ASPECT RATIO FORMATS

Most films today are shot in either a 1.85:1 or a 2.35:1 aspect ratio. The most common aspect ratio for motion pictures is 1.85:1, or standardized, nonanamorphic films. Films produced in the 1.85:1 aspect ratio are personal films that include comedies, dramas, and many animated films.

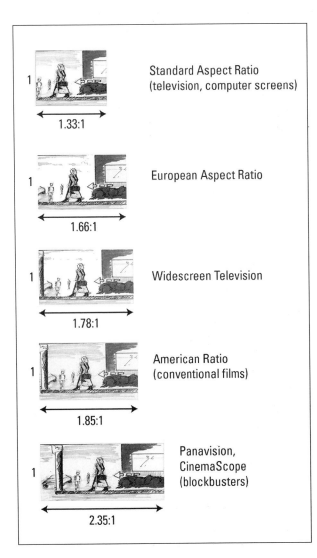

If someone were to describe a film as "epic" or "monumental," chances are the film was shot using a 2.35:1 aspect ratio, which included Panavision and other anamorphic films. Some films shot using the 2.35:1 aspect ratio include *Gladiator, The Lord of the Rings,* and *Braveheart.*

A standard television screen has a 1.33:1 aspect ratio, but many televisions being manufactured today have a wider aspect ratio of 1.78:1 (commonly referred to as a 16:9 ratio). This new standard was introduced into the broadcast market because of consumer preference for a wider screen. A 16:9 screen contains more of the image's content and enhances the movie experience. Since the 16:9 aspect ratio is closer to the theatrical screen ratio of 1.85:1, when cropped for widescreen television, the theatrical aspect ratio of 1.85:1 does not lose noticeable picture information.

figure **2-10**

Various aspect ratios.
Drawing courtesy of Art Jaruphaiboon

The difference between the width and height of a movie screen is much greater than the difference between the width and height of a standard television screen. For example, if you were to show *Gladiator* on a conventional television screen without altering the image, you would lose about 20 percent of the image on each end. Fortunately, there are techniques that can adjust for the proportional difference between motion picture images and television screens.

Pan & Scan

The industry was once again in a predicament when their movies sold to television and home video, and had to be cropped from their original size to fit the 1.33:1 screen shape of television. In the early 1960s, Twentieth Century Fox developed the pan & scan process that resizes widescreen movies to fit within a 1.33:1 aspect ratio. The pan & scan process locates the "center of interest" of an image and fits it into the space available for standard television. For example, if you have two characters at either end of a shot within a widescreen version, one or both characters will be lost when it is displayed in a standard 4:3 frame.

figure | 2-11 |

Pan & scan.

Using pan & scan, a video technician will re-edit the shot by either cutting back and forth between a conversation to follow the action, or by cropping the image according to the center of interest. A drawback to pan & scan is that audiences only see a portion of the image on their television sets, which alters the way the director intended audiences to view the film. For instance, a 1.85:1 aspect ratio will lose about 25 percent of the film image, whereas a 2.35:1 aspect ratio loses almost 45-50 percent.

Letterboxing

For most directors, pan & scan was not a viable alternative to showcasing their films on television. Many banded together to ensure that their compositions would not be manipulated under pan & scan. Instead, directors opted for letterboxing, which maintains a film's original aspect ratio, preserving the image as it was originally seen in a movie theater. Letterboxed images, however, do not fill the entire screen. Rather, the picture is centered along the horizontal plane and shrunk to fit the shape of a television screen. This results in empty space above and below the image.

figure | 2-12 |

Letterboxing.

Neutral Space

Preserved Picture

Neutral Space

Letterbox Image

? DID YOU KNOW One of the first directors to use letterboxing was Woody Allen for his 1979 film *Manhattan*.

CALCULATING ASPECT RATIOS FOR STORYBOARDS

When working on a project, you will need to calculate storyboard frames in proportion to the aspect ratio for the film. Let's say, for example, the aspect ratio for a film is 1.85:1. First, you must decide at what height you want to render your storyboards.

Determining frame height is based on either the preference of the director, or how many frames you work best with on a page. Once the frame height is chosen, calculate its width. If, in this case, you have decided on a frame height of 4 inches, you would multiply 1.85 by 4 to obtain a film frame width of 7.4 inches.

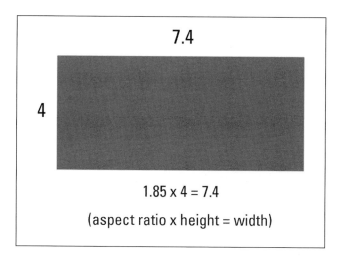

figure | 2-13 |

Aspect Ratio x Height = Width.

You may also calculate the aspect ratio for a film or animation if you already know the height and width of the screen. Divide the screen's width by its height to calculate its aspect ratio. For example, a screen width of 4 divided by a screen height of 3 is equal to an aspect ratio of 1.33:1.

CHAPTER SUMMARY

The modern storyboard arose out of Disney Studios, but early filmmakers such as Sergi Eisenstein and Cecil B. DeMille were creating detailed sketches to help determine the staging of scenes and camera placement. The real need for the storyboard came from the animation industry. In animation's infancy, there were no story departments. Rather, the studios relied on their animators to generate stories based on gags. This changed when Disney formed the first story department in the 1930s, which was lead by Ted Sears. Gagmen and artists would work together, sketching out story ideas for upcoming cartoons. The first animation to use the modern storyboard was the short *The Three Little Pigs*. Live-action directors who adapted storyboards to their projects include Alfred Hitchcock and Orson Welles.

In the early years of film, the aspect ratio was 1.33:1, which is a square shape. As film matured, and received competition from television, the aspect ratio was adjusted to reflect wider screens. Two popular widescreen formats in the 1950s were Cinerama and CinemaScope. These two formats eventually gave way to Panavision, and the standard aspect ratios of 1.85:1 and 2.35:1.

The widescreen format had some trouble when films began to be shown on television. The difference between the width and height in an average movie image is much greater than the difference between the width and height of a standard television screen. The industry came up with the technique of pan & scan, which resizes the image by finding the center of interest and cropping. The more favorable letterbox technique shrinks the image to fit the screen rather than losing any parts of the image.

Before determining compositional elements of the storyboard frame, an artist must establish the shape of the storyboard panel. Many artists work within the aspect ratio used to photograph a film. The aspect ratio for a film or animation refers to the height and width of a screen.

in review

1. What studio was responsible for the modern storyboard?

2. What role did Saul Bass play in the creation of the shower sequence in *Psycho*?

3. What directors use storyboards?

4. How did Dave Fleischer contribute to story development at Fleischer Studios?

5. How do you calculate aspect ratios?

6. Why was Cinerama introduced to the public?

7. Why did the film industry slightly adjust the aspect ratio of films from 1.33:1 to 1.37:1 in the early days of film?

8. What is the difference between pan & scan and letterboxing?

9. What are two standard aspect ratios used in films today?

exercises

1. Aspect ratios for film and animation are 1.33:1 for television, 1.85:1 for standard, and 2.35:1 for blockbuster movies. Calculate the panel size according to each of these aspect ratios and create a cutout for each.

2. Next, acquire storyboards rendered in a 2.35:1 aspect ratio (see appendix C for a list of art books that feature storyboards). Overlay the 1.33:1 and 1.85:1 aspect ratio cutouts over each panel that you just created. Notice what elements fall outside the cutout for each panel.

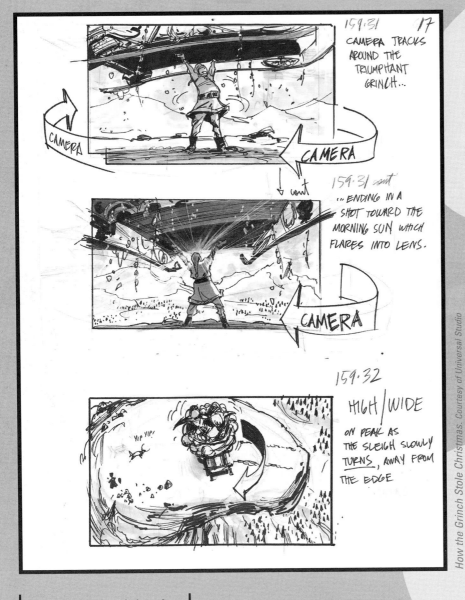

159:31   17
CAMERA TRACKS
AROUND THE
TRIUMPHANT
GRINCH...

CAMERA

CAMERA

↓ cont

159.31 cont
"...ENDING IN A
SHOT TOWARD THE
MORNING SUN WHICH
FLARES INTO LENS.

CAMERA

159.32
HIGH/WIDE
ON PEAK AS
THE SLEIGH SLOWLY
TURNS, AWAY FROM
THE EDGE

YIP YIP!

How the Grinch Stole Christmas. Courtesy of Universal Studio

| fundamentals of the shot |

3

objectives

Understand the difference between scenes and shots

Visualize a scene in terms of framing, angles, and movement

Understand illustrating camera and character movement with directional arrows

introduction

Film, animation, and gaming are a visual language, and to successfully communicate each media's objectives for a project, a director or designer needs to know what to say with each individual shot within a scene. Carefully planned shots can heighten audience reaction to a project, but if those shots are haphazardly chosen, the spectator may walk away confused. Planning what the audience should see can make the difference in a project's success or failure.

This chapter introduces terminology specific to the shot, including camera framing, camera angles, and movement. Illustrating camera direction for character and camera movement with directional arrows is also discussed.

FUNDAMENTALS OF THE SHOT

SHOT DESCRIPTIONS

Before undertaking a storyboarding job, you must first understand how screen stories are broken down into sequences, scenes, and shots.

The most basic unit of production is the shot, which is a continuous view filmed from one perspective. Think of it this way: anytime the camera is turned on, films something, and then is turned off, you have a new shot. If the camera setup is changed to show a different viewpoint, this also constitutes a new shot. Scenes, on the other hand, are a combination of shots of the action that takes place in one location or setting. Lastly, all screenplays are made up of sequences, which are a combination of several scenes. A sequence might start inside a church, for instance, and continue to the cemetery. The director of film, animation, or video gaming sequences is responsible for determining how sequences should look and feel, right down to each individual action within a shot. This is not an easy task, considering that the average number of shots to plan a production is about 1,200.

There are several factors that influence the director's decision-making process regarding shot setup. One of those factors is to capture the best viewpoint of the action that is both visually stimulating and easy to comprehend by the audience. Mood is also a determining factor when capturing the action of a shot. Position the camera high up in a shot, for example, and the audience might feel a character's degradation. Lower the camera and you get the opposite effect. If a scene describes a little boy in hysterics after losing his dog, you might use a close-up to show his grief. As you read the script, you should begin to visualize what the film frame looks like.

As objectives are clearly defined for a project, you need three important pieces of information:

- How should the shot be **framed**?
- What camera **angles** best express the mood of the shot?
- Is camera **movement** in the shot?

Camera Framing

Frame size is based on how close or far a subject is from the camera, but how does a director decide what is the best viewing area when planning shots?

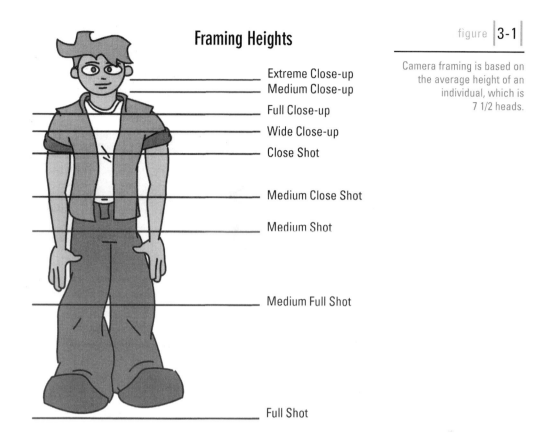

Framing Heights

Extreme Close-up
Medium Close-up
Full Close-up
Wide Close-up
Close Shot
Medium Close Shot
Medium Shot
Medium Full Shot
Full Shot

figure | 3-1 |

Camera framing is based on the average height of an individual, which is 7 1/2 heads.

Project goals and what media it plays out in must be confirmed before the actual planning of a project begins. The overall style for a drama, for instance, may move slower and include more close-ups than an epic adventure film that includes wider shots of sweeping views.

In regard to media, the frame size for commercials, video games, and industrial videos is much smaller than film. Therefore, you might opt for framing the action closer for a television storyboard. In contrast, panoramic shots, such as those used in *Gladiator* and *The Lord of the Rings*, simply lose their power on the small screen and are best served for theatrical programs.

Many directors may begin shot selection by applying a basic formula to planning scenes. This formula includes starting with an establishing shot, then moving in closer to the action in increments, as listed below:

- Establish a setting with a long shot to show characters in relation to the background.

- Move in to a medium shot to introduce the interaction between characters. The closer you go, the more personal the story becomes.

- Employ close-ups to underscore a character's personality.

- Come back to a long shot or medium shot to reorient the viewer.

figure | 3-2 |

The basic formula for a scene begins with an establishing shot and moves closer to the action in stages.

Many directors move well beyond this rudimentary guideline by experimenting with contrasting and repetitious framing. For example, a director may contrast a wide shot with a close-up, followed by several medium shots.

As a storyboard artist, you must understand the specifics of framing and how it influences the tone of a production.

Extreme Long Shot (ELS)

The extreme long shot establishes the context for the shots that follow by setting up the location. Extreme long shots are typically used to depict the vastness of an area, such as a city skyline, a suburban neighborhood, or a farm. We typically see extreme long shots as the opener of a film or scene. Watch many Western films, and you will likely find an establishing long shot of the landscape.

figure | 3-3 |

Extreme long shot.

Long Shot (LS)

Also called the wide shot, the long shot shows the location (where are we?), the subject (who is there?), and the action (what is happening?). This is one of the most important shots because it establishes the elements of a scene. The long shot may depict the openness of a soccer field, gymnasium, or ranch. Such shots set the mood of a scene and set up character positions within the environment.

figure | 3-4 |

Long shot.

Full Shot (FS)

This shot frames the entire height of a person, with the head near the top of the frame and the feet near the bottom. What you want to avoid when creating a full shot is cutting off part of the subject's head or feet. A full shot provides focus on an actor's body language and posture.

figure | 3-5 |

Full shot.

Medium Shot (MS)

The medium shot frames an individual from either the waist or the knees up, showing the audience just enough to feel as if they are looking at the whole subject. Medium shots are used most frequently for dialogue scenes between two or three individuals. Facial expressions and gestures are shown, and there is just enough background visible to provide information on the location.

Medium shots are often used in television because it is a "close up" medium. Medium shots are also used quite frequently in film because it places the audience at a "normal" distance right after a scene is established. In the basic setup, the medium shot is usually presented right after the long shot.

figure |3-6|

Medium shot.

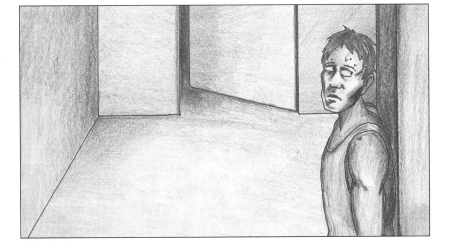

Close-Up Shot (CU)

There are variations of the close-up shot, but the most basic shows a character from the shoulders to the top of the head. Close-ups are used quite regularly in television, particularly in soap operas, creating a close connection between the audience and a character. The intimacy of close-ups focuses on the most expressive part of a person—the face. The close-up is also great for isolating a significant detail. For instance, a gloved hand turning a doorknob might provide the audience with necessary clues.

figure |3-7|

Close-up shot.

Extreme Close-Up Shot (ECU)

Extreme close-up shots are used to elevate tension, mystery, or emotion by filling the frame with an image. This shot is designed to show the detail of a face, such as a mouth, or the detail of an object, such as a doorknob. Extreme close-ups are also wonderful for showing emotion. Take for instance a father presenting his young son with a new puppy. Cutting to an extreme close-up of the boy's enthusiastic face lets the viewer know that he is happy with the dog.

figure |3-8|

Extreme close-up shot.

Single Shot

The single shot is the most basic shot because it focuses on one person in the frame. Single shots are often medium shots and close-ups.

figure |3-9|

Single shot.

figure | 3-10 |

Two shot.

figure | 3-11 |

Insert shot.

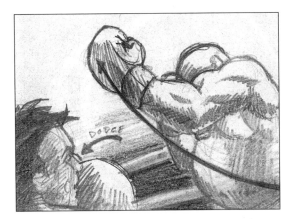

figure | 3-12 |

A low-angle shot dramatizes the power of one fighter over another.

Two Shot

An interesting shot is the two shot, in which two characters occupy the frame. There are several variations of the two shot that include positioning characters face to face, placing one character slightly behind another to create depth, and turning one character slightly toward the camera while the other is turned inward. Two shots are often used to convey a conversation, whether an argument or discussion, between characters.

Insert Shot

This shot is usually a close-up of an action or an object that is inserted into the main action of a master scene. A photograph resting on a mantle piece is considered an insert shot.

Camera Angles

Camera angles grab our attention by creating dynamic scenes. They often influence how an audience responds to a character or situation on the screen. Consider the dangerous confrontation between two heavyweight boxers, Ray and Jake, in *Raging Bull.* In one scene, there is a low-angle shot of Ray pummeling Jake, followed by a high-angle shot of a bloodied and battered Jake against the ropes. The low-angle of Ray, coupled with a high-angle of Jake, shows Ray's dominance and Jake's insignificance.

Camera angles also create depth within a frame. Let's say you adjust the camera angle to a three-quarter view of a character. By angling the camera, the director creates depth between the foreground and background elements.

High-Angle Shot

A camera placed higher than the subject (but not directly overhead) and tilted downward often evokes an emotional response from the audience. High-angled shots provide the audience with variety and often suggest a character's insignificance in the world. A location, or perhaps another person, often dwarfs the object or character.

High-angle shots are also used to create an aesthetically pleasing frame. Take for instance a high-angle shot of a roller coaster. Framing the roller coaster from above provides the audience with details of both the subjects and the environment.

figure | 3-13 |

High-angle shot.

figure | 3-14 |

Low-angle shot.

Low-Angle Shot

A camera placed lower than the subject and tilted upward often produces shots that are visually exciting to an audience.

A low-angle shot of the President, for instance, might inspire awe from the audience, whereas a low-angle shot of a killer makes him appear menacing. Characters of power are often shot at a slightly lower angle to suggest their dominance. Low-angle shots also work well when one character is positioned higher in the frame than the other.

Eye-Level Shot

This is a fairly neutral shot in which the camera is positioned at eye level with a character. The camera looks the character directly in the eye, when the audience is meant to identify with the character as an equal.

figure **3-15**

Eye-level shot.

"As you're drawing you're thinking about the look of the scene, how the camera moves...you get a sense of the pace, the characters, and it's my way of doing my homework."

Tony Scott, Director
Spy Game

Bird's-Eye View

A bird's-eye view takes a slightly different approach from the high-angle shot by positioning the camera directly overhead of the action. The bird's-eye view allows the audience to look down on the buildings and bridges within a city, or perhaps a football stadium.

figure **3-16**

Bird's-eye view.

Canted Shot

A canted shot, also called the Dutch shot, views an image off-center, or tilted, so that the subject appears to be diagonal and off-balance. This effect creates an unsettling feeling with the audience. We often see canted angles within scenes that portray characters as unhinged, violent, and out of control. Canted shots are used extensively in horror films, psychological dramas, and crime pictures.

figure | 3-17 |

Canted shot.

Tilt Shot

A tilt shot is done with a fixed camera that moves on its vertical axis, tilting up or down. For example, tilting up or down the side of a skyscraper conveys a feeling of height. A tilt shot is often used to reveal a subject by degrees, such as showing a character's feet first as the camera travels up the body to the face.

figure | 3-18 |

Tilt shot.

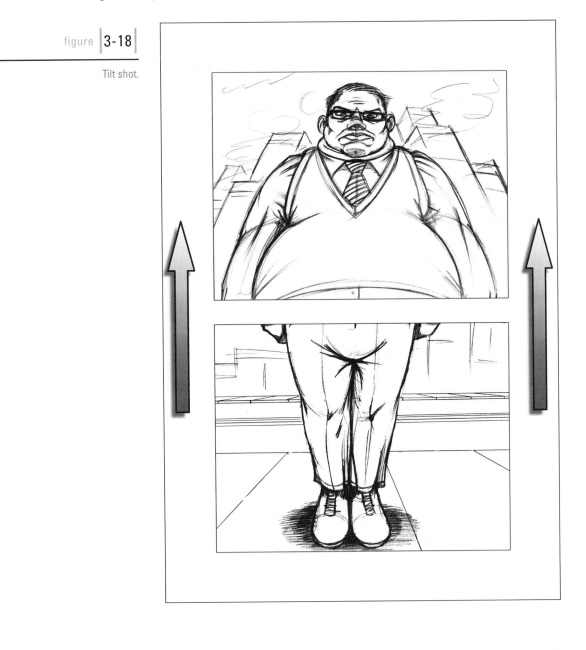

Three-Quarter Shot

Also known as a forty-five degree shot, the three-quarter shot provides the strongest composition by positioning the camera between a frontal angle and a profile shot. This shot is used most often because it provides for depth between the foreground and background elements.

figure 3-19

Three-quarter shot.

Frontal Shot

The camera is positioned directly in front of the subject matter in frontal shots, which are flat, but when used as close-ups, they often convey a feeling of intimacy. Frontal shots are also used for subjective shots, which connect the character to the audience. In the comedy *Wayne's World,* the director employs frontal shots as Wayne talks directly to the camera, interacting with the audience.

figure 3-20

Frontal shot.

Profile Shot

Also known as a side shot, this angle is composed directly from the side of an object or person at eye level.

figure 3-21

Profile shot.

Over-the-Shoulder Shot (OTS)

This shot positions the camera over the shoulder of one character, revealing part of the backside of their head and shoulders in the foreground, and focuses on the character facing the camera in the background. Over-the-shoulder shots are commonly used for framing conversations between two people and are often used in tandem with reaction shots.

figure 3-22

Over-the-shoulder shot.

Camera Movement

The image fades up, revealing a couple cheek-to-cheek in a medium close shot. The camera pulls back to reveal the couple dancing alongside several other individuals. The camera then spins around the dance floor, creating a sense of dynamic motion, which is part of the storytelling process. When there is plenty of action between characters or objects, the camera may remain static or move amongst the characters. Where there is minimal action in a scene, camera movement creates energy by moving within the environment.

How would you represent such movement within a two-dimensional space such as a storyboard panel? To create movement within the storyboard frame, an artist must understand the use of directional arrows, which indicate the movement of the camera, as well as the action of characters and objects within a frame. They can show, for example, a very simple motion of a man picking up a soda can, or a complex tracking shot of an escaped convict running through the woods. We will discuss directional arrows and extended frames further in Chapter 4.

figure 3-23a

Camera movement.
Courtesy of David Phillips

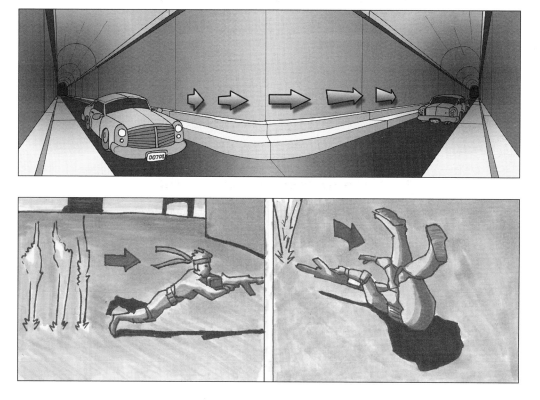

figure 3-23b

Directional arrows show the movement of the soldier.

Crane Shot

A camera positioned on a crane can swoop down or up, covering great distances and producing unusual camera angles. Depending on the context, the effect can be soothing, exhilarating, or menacing.

figure | 3-24 |

Crane shot.

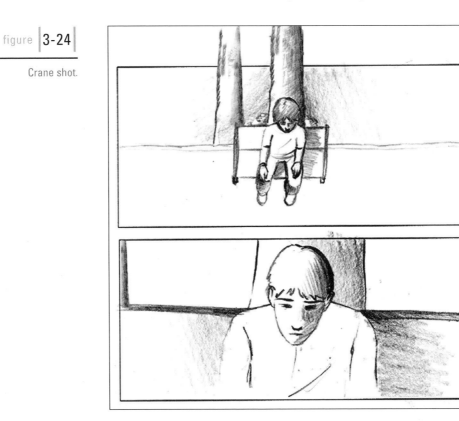

Crane shots are most exciting when they are used within a three-dimensional environment. Whereas a traditional camera is limited to where it can move, a virtual camera can go anywhere. One of the most recognized shots using a "virtual" camera is from *Titanic* when Jack stands at the bow of the ship with his arms spread wide. The camera swoops backward, then rises inches from the funnels of the ship, creating a breathtaking shot. Such a shot is impossible using a traditional camera.

Pan Shot

A fixed camera pivots on its axis, turning from left to right for the purpose of following the action within a shot. A pan moves across an image while maintaining equal distance from it. The pan often directs the attention of the spectator from one part of a location to another part.

Many directors use pans to establish a location, such as the vastness of a country estate. When a pan is made rapidly, it is called a swish pan. This is when the camera makes a dramatic shift from one object or location to another. You can see the swish pan on such televisions shows as *The Practice*, which uses the swish pan to dramatically show a location shift.

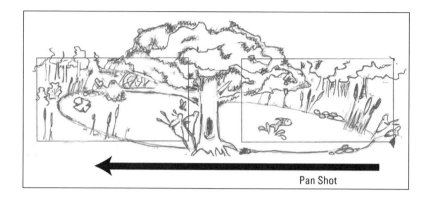

Pan Shot

figure |3-25|

Pan shot.

Dolly Shot

A dolly shot is where a camera on a dolly or a camera truck moves toward a subject (dolly-in) or moves away from a subject (dolly-out). A dolly shot may establish a character lounging by the pool, and then move in close to establish the character's facial movements and gestures.

> | **TIP** |
>
> Watch the way a group of friends toss a baseball. Imagine how the camera would capture the motion from different perspectives.

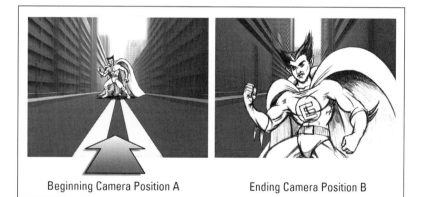

Beginning Camera Position A   Ending Camera Position B

figure |3-26|

Dolly-in shot.

D.W. Griffith was the pioneer of camera movement with his film *Birth of a Nation*.

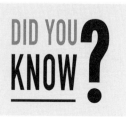

Tracking Shot

A tracking shot is similar to a dolly shot, but instead of moving in and out, the camera tracks alongside of the object or person. Tracking shots allow the audience to follow characters as they walk and talk to each other.

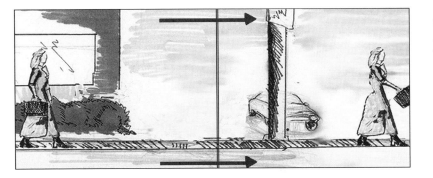

figure |3-27|

Tracking shot.

Zoom

The camera stays stationary as the focal length of a lens zooms in or out. When a shot zooms in—also called a push shot—it gets "tighter." When the shot slowly zooms out—also called a pull shot—it gets "looser." Zooms may start out as an extreme close-up, as in figure 3-28, and zoom out to a medium shot to reveal the reason for the character's fear.

figure |3-28|

Zoom out.

Steadicam® Shot

A Steadicam® is a camera that is mounted in a harness, which a cameraman wears around his body. Using the Steadicam®, the cameraman can follow a character, or object, almost anywhere with amazing smoothness. One of the most famous Steadicam® shots lasted for three minutes in the gangster picture *Goodfellas*. The shot begins with Henry Hill giving money to a car attendant, and tracks him walking through the restaurant to his table, as friends greet him.

Zolly Shot

Alfred Hitchcock was famous for the zolly shot, which is a dolly shot in combination with a zoom. In *Jaws*, Spielberg used the zolly effect when Brody witnesses a little boy eaten by the shark. Brody is sitting on the beach and as the camera dollies toward him, the zoom lens is pulled back. Spielberg used this shot to communicate Brody's sudden surprise and disorientation.

figure | 3-29 |

Zolly shot.

Camera Perspective

There are three perspectives to consider when planning a project: objective, point of view (POV), and subjective. Each perspective needs to be considered, including how they should be framed, angle of view, and movement.

Objective Shot

In an objective shot, the camera is placed in a neutral position. The audience does not take the perspective of any of the characters, but rather observes the action from the sidelines. Objective shots give the audience the best, unbiased view of the action. We often see these types of shots in documentaries, situation comedies, and interview shows as the camera takes on the role of unobtrusive observer.

Point of View Shot

The point of view shot (POV) is from the perspective of a specific character. Placing the camera near a character whose viewpoint is being depicted creates point of view shots. These types of shots usually increase audience involvement because we are seeing events

figure | 3-30 |

With an objective shot the viewer is passive, watching the action from the sidelines.

unfold from a specific character's viewpoint. Audiences identify much more closely with the action because it is as if we are standing next to the character in question.

Point of view shots are often filmed as over-the-shoulder shots, where we see each player's POV. This is often the case when staging the hero of a film or animation. It is easier to identify with the hero if we see what he sees, rather than as an objective bystander watching the action unfold.

figure |3-31|

The point of view shot is from the perspective of a specific character.

Subjective Shot

The subjective camera is the most personal and interactive of any of the previous viewpoints. Subjective shots are when the camera trades places with an on-screen character, allowing the viewer to see the action through that character's eyes. The audience experiences what the character experiences. We often see subjective shots in video games. For instance, a player might be the character that looks through the riflescope to pinpoint its target.

figure |3-32|

The camera trades places with the character in subjective shots.

A subjective shot also occurs when an on-screen character looks into the lens and addresses the audience. A popular film that used this technique is the 1980's hit *Ferris Bueller's Day Off*. When Ferris addresses the camera, he draws the audience in, making them feel a part of the story and not just a spectator.

CHAPTER SUMMARY

Before the storyboard job commences, every artist must have a clear understanding of the grammar of film, which includes sequences, scenes, and shots. The most basic unit of production is the shot, which is a continuous view filmed from one perspective. Each time the camera position is changed, you have a new shot. Scenes are a collection of shots that tell a story from beginning to end. Sequences are a collection of scenes that move a story forward.

Shots are blocked according to camera framing, angles, and movement. Camera framing is based on the distance from the subject to the camera. It is wise to learn not only how to frame shots, but also the meaning behind framing a shot. For instance, a medium shot is often used to show the interaction between two characters, whereas close-ups are more intimate.

Camera angles add dynamism to a frame and often grab the audience's attention. A high angle, for example, often suggests insignificance or even isolation.

Movement is defined by either camera or character movement within a frame. Since a storyboard panel is defined within a two-dimensional space, artists must use directional arrows to express movement.

in review

1. Explain three camera techniques for creating storyboards.

2. What is a two shot? When should two shots be used?

3. What is a canted angle? What types of films use canted shots?

4. When should close-ups be used?

5. What type of shot would you use to establish two people arguing? Why?

6. Who made the zolly shot famous? How does it work?

7. When would you utilize a tilt-up shot?

exercises

1. Creating a dynamic story through shot selection

   Break down the following scene by blocking characters and the camera. How do you intend to visually tell the story? Compose each shot utilizing camera framing, angles, and movement.

   a. Exterior: Center City Park

   b. A man jogs at a leisurely pace.

   c. An out of control rollerblader enters the park across from the jogger.

   d. The jogger passes a couple walking their dog.

   e. The jogger stops to pet the dog before continuing on.

   f. The rollerblader intersects the path of the jogger, and trips over the jogger's foot.

   g. The rollerblader collides with a park bench.

2. Analyzing a scene

Scenes are made up of shots that show camera framing, angles, and
movement. This exercise will help you to understand shot selection
by the director.

Pick a scene from a film that has twenty to thirty shots. Watch the scene
several times. On your last viewing, pause your DVD or VCR on each shot.
Write down a complete shot description, including framing, camera angle,
and camera movement, if applicable. Pay strict attention to what catches your
eye. What do you think the shot is supposed to convey in the overall scheme of
the scene?

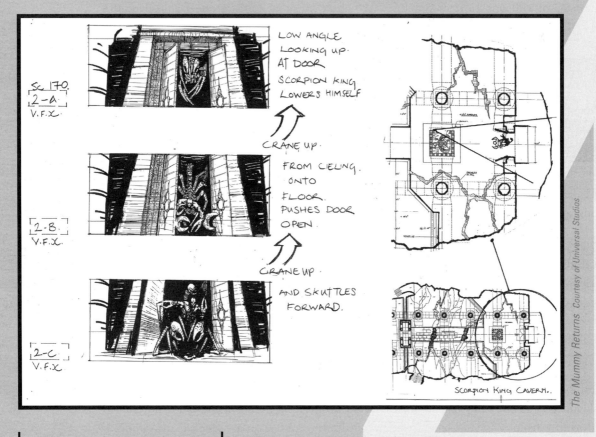

SC 170.
2-A
V.F.X.

2-B.
V.F.X.

2-C.
V.F.X.

LOW ANGLE
LOOKING UP.
AT DOOR
SCORPION KING
LOWERS HIMSELF

CRANE UP.

FROM CIELING.
ONTO
FLOOR.
PUSHES DOOR
OPEN.

CRANE UP.
AND SKUTTLES
FORWARD.

SCORPION KING CAVERN.

from script to final storyboard

objectives

Understand the function of the shooting script, shot list, and overhead diagram

Demonstrate camera and character movement

Understand the psychological impact of choosing specific camera angles, framing, and movement

Define the storyboard approach from creating thumbnails to roughs to final storyboards

introduction

Words on a page come to life in the form of visuals, whether we are reading a romance novel, a short story, or an animation script. If a screenplay indicates a little boy pretending to be a pirate, for example, each of us may have a different picture of what the scene looks like. By storyboarding the scene, everyone involved in the production will be on the same page for how it should be executed.

figure | 4-1 |

Visualizing individual shots of a story convey emotion, such as a knight slaying the fearsome dragon to save the fair maiden.

Courtesy of J. Allen McFadden

FROM SCRIPT TO FINAL STORYBOARD

The storyboarding process begins with the breakdown of the script into component pieces. Visualizing individual shots may seem uncomplicated, but when those shots are translated into scenes that tell a visually dynamic story and convey emotion, the job becomes much tougher. Preparing a project should not be taken lightly or considered a hindrance to the creative process.

The complexity of the storyboards often depends on the requirements of the director. Martin Scorsese, the director of such films as *The Gangs of New York* and *Goodfellas*, for instance, creates simple drawings to show how scenes should be blocked. Many directors create detailed storyboards, such as those created by David Fincher for *Fight Club*. No matter what the director's style, one of the most important elements of a storyboard is that it gives the production crew the opportunity to see what is necessary to do their jobs effectively.

This chapter looks specifically at the planning stage, which includes the creation of overheads, shot lists, and storyboards, which are the fabric for how shots are evaluated and arranged to tell a story.

THE SHOOTING SCRIPT

The shooting script is the finalized screenplay that has received the "green light" for production. Once approved, it falls to the director, who analyzes each scene to understand how one shot flows into the next, and which scenes require new camera setups. Components of the

THE STORYBOARD ARTIST AT WORK

Warren Drummond

© Photo courtesy of Andrew Orth

Q. How did you become interested in storyboarding?

A. I was always a cartoonist and started working for magazines like *The Source*, a hip-hop publication, and *Glamour*, a fashion monthly. When I was struggling, I realized that storyboards combined my love of film and comics, and I could get paid!

Q. What are several of your career highlights?

A. They would have to be working on *Star Wars—Episode 2: Attack of the Clones*, *A Beautiful Mind*, *Antwone Fisher*, and *2 Fast 2 Furious*. The *Star Wars* job lasted a week, but what a week it was working at the Skywalker Ranch. *A Beautiful Mind* allowed me to work with Ron Howard, one of the most talented directors and all around nice guys. Ron let myself and the other storyboard artist, Brick Mason, design shots, and then he would adjust them to his liking. Denzel Washington was new to directing and very open on *Antwone Fisher*. He never let me feel like any of the suggestions I made were invaluable.

2 Fast 2 Furious was my third film with my close friend John Singleton. John is very prepared and comes with a shot list, which he has worked out in his head. I had more responsibility because I was working with all the producers on the film.

Q. What has been your most challenging project to date?

A. My most challenging project would have to be *2 Fast 2 Furious*. I was the storyboard artist who worked on the project from the beginning of preproduction until the very end. The job took me from Los Angeles to Miami and the hours were very long. It is probably my most cherished job because the crew made me feel like I was a vital part of the production. Working with a great crew really helps.

Q. How much influence do you have with a director?

A. My influence with a director depends on what they need, how confident they are, and how open they are to suggestions. John Singleton knows what he wants and writes a detailed shot list, but he leaves the door open for another person's ideas. Ron Howard does not like to shot list his films, and will often let the storyboard artist make a pass at a scene, which he will then review and change. Ron is very receptive, but he will shape the final vision.

New directors, or directors that aren't as strong with shot selection, will take an artist's advice more than others. Of course, there are always the occasional directors who are ironclad in their decisions, and you are their robot. But I would have to say that if there is trust between director and artist, and they know you have their best interests in mind, they could be quite receptive.

Q. How many panels do you sketch per day?

A. On my very brief stint on *Star Wars: Episode 2*, the requirement was at least fourteen highly detailed frames per day. On another film, with looser frames, it may be twenty to thirty, or in crunch time fifty very sketchy frames.

Q. How many weeks will you work on a project?

A. The time spent working on a film is dependent on the size of a project. Jobs can last from two days to months to a year or more. It depends on if the movie has many action sequences and what the budget is for the project.

Q. What advice would you give students interested in the field of storyboarding?

A. If your goal is to be a good storyboard artist, you must have a grasp for drawing people, objects, and perspective. This is a deadline industry, so you must be able to draw very fast.

You must know film storytelling, which is similar to but much different than comics. My advice is to watch classic films and look at the director's choices in terms of shot selection, when to cut, and how they put shots together to form a scene. If your goal is to storyboard for commercials, analyze them, but know that they are different than feature films or television because the main goal is to sell a product.

Q. How do you get hired for a job?

A. Most of my jobs are from referrals and relationships. I got the *Star Wars* job from a relationship I developed with stunt coordinator Nick Gillard on *Shaft*. Sometimes I'll work on a project, and the production designer or other crewmember will remember me, and bring me on board for a new job.

I've also gotten gigs from sending out my resume and sample book and making the calls and mailings, although this is a very hard and time-consuming process.

shooting script include camera framing and angles, lighting notations, and character blocking. This analysis helps the director to determine how the production will be shot, along with its schedule and budget.

Each scene of a shooting script is given a "scene number," and includes a brief description of the camera action and framing for each shot. Nothing should be specified in the shooting script that is beyond the resources of the production. Another element of the shooting script is visualizing how many special effects and stunts are required.

SHOT LIST

Once a screenplay goes into production, the director creates the shot list, which is a written list of the intended shots for each scene. The list describes important elements that are necessary for a successful production. The major elements of the shot list include:

INTERIORS AND EXTERIORS FOR "THE NIGHT OF THE HUNTER"

EXTERIORS

Miscellaneous helicopter shots above Ohio River country, including:
Descending shot centering a deserted, small-town house
""   "'   "   the Harper home
"   "   "   towards a city (Louisville or Cincinnati)
beside a much widened River; night.
A shot showing Cresap's Landing in relation to the Harper house.
Shots of small river towns will feature church steeples.

Also: Miscellaneous helicopter shots showing children in boat in River Sequence;
including a shot pulling up & away —night -- as they fall asleep, drifting. Their
boat to remain visible — presumably on moonlit water -- as they continue drifting
downstream.

And possibly: a helicopter shot linking Preacher, riding down a riverside road,
and the children in their boat, a bend or two further downstream, beyond his seeing.

The deserted house, featuring: tree in side-yard, with broken swing; cellar door;
small portion of cellar in down-shot.

The Harper home, featuring: a grape arbor, in handy view of the road; a gas lamp
in the front yard (see Grubb's drawing); a somewhat uneven dirt road which runs
one way into open country and the other, into Peacock Alley (main street of
Cresap's Landing); River, paralleling road, near front of house.

Peacock Alley (Cresap's Landing), featuring:
Jander's Livery Stable (with brick wall for gallows drawing)
The Spoon's Ice Cream Parlor
Lane down to River and Uncle Birdie's (in clear relation to Spoon's Parlor)
Miz Cunningham's
Mamie Ernest — Room & Board
and, possibly:
A swinging, creaking, wooden key in front of a small shop
Ben's unmarked grave, in the town churchyard
and, certainly:
A small neat white Church, open to a grassy bank sloping gently to the River

Uncle Birdie's; and establishing Ben Harper's skiff near by, and clear relation
to Spoon's Parlor and Peacock Alley. Maybe: shanty-boats in b.g.

Alley for side-exit from Burlesque House
A stretch of city street in that poor and hard neighborhood, featuring:
entry to a small and poor hotel

Small portion of Prison Courtyard as Hangman and his companion leave

Street down which Hangman walks home

Front of Hangman's home

```
REEL ONE PART A            "THE NIGHT OF THE HUNTER"            PAGE 5.

A1597   49.   EXT. FARMYARD - DAY - CU - Ben talking        3-7     599-8

 600    50.   CU - John taking oath                         3-4     602-12

 603    51.   MS - the two SIDE ANGLE - John repeats       12-14    615-10
              promise, Ben grabs his hand and shakes it
              then turns looking o.s.

 616    52.   CU - Pearl seated with doll - she nods        4-0     615-10
              her head.

 616    53.   LS - State troopers moving from cars to       4-11    620-5
              FG with guns in hand.

 621    54.   CU - John re-acting very frightened           2-2     622-7

 623    55.   MLS - John and Ben SIDE ANGLE - troopers     12-4     634-11
              approaching cautiously in BG. Ben backs
              up towards troopers with gun in hand -
              trooper grabs gun from his hand as others
              rush in.

 635    56.   MS - Trooper by two others holding Ben's      1-4     635-15
              arms.

 636    57.   MCS - John re-acts and puts hands to his      1-4     637-3
              stomach with sickly expression - he speaks.

 638    58.   MS - Troopers take Ben to ground holding      2-3     639-6
              his hands behind him, CAMERA PANNING.
              One starts to hand-cuff Ben.

 640    59.   CU - John re-acting - he speaks               1-7     640-13

 641    60.   MS - Troopers with Ben on ground - they      1-13     642-10
              struggle as one holds gun on him.

 643    61.   CU - John re-acts - he yells and is about     2-1     644-11
              to cry.

 645    62.   MLS - Troopers with Ben on ground - one      3-10     648-5
              kneels down and hand-cuffs him as others
              hold  guns

 649    63.   CU - John watching o.s. in horror            1-12     650-1

 651    64.   MLS - Troopers take Ben handcuffed to BG      6-14     656-15

 657    65.   LS - John watching o.s. as Willa runs in     5-13     662-12
              and stops - Pearl runs in to Willa, they
              watch o.s. to FG.
```

figure | 4-3 |

Night of the Hunter shot list.
Courtesy of the Library of Congress

- Camera framing: What is the distance from the camera to the subject?

- Camera angle: The angle the camera is placed in relation to the subject.

- Script description: Written notations that are transcribed from the script into the shot list. Script notes assist the director in identifying the placement of the shot in relation to what is happening in the screenplay.

Other considerations when creating the shot list are props and budgetary constraints. If a film's budget is tight, the director is not likely to plan ambitious camera moves that require crane and/or dolly rentals. The more detail the director puts into compiling the shot list, the more likely the shoot will run smoothly—saving both time and money.

Shot Selection: Practical, Aesthetic, and Psychological Factors

When determining shot selection, there are certain criteria to consider, including practical, aesthetic, and psychological factors. Practical considerations may include from what character's viewpoint the story is being told. If the viewpoint is subjective and a character talks directly to the camera, for instance, frontal shots may dominate. Over-the-shoulder shots may dictate a point of view perspective. Other practical considerations include basic shot selections. For example, an establishing shot is necessary anytime a new location or setting is introduced because it acclimates the audience to where they are and what is happening in a scene. Suppose you want to create a scene where the villain places a bomb under a car in a parking lot. There are many shot choices available to create such a dramatic scene. You may decide to open the scene with a wide shot of the parking lot to establish the location.

But what if you want to start the scene with a close shot of the bomb and then cut to the villain, as in figure 4-4? Starting with a close-up is a common technique and often an effective one. Slowly revealing information increases intrigue for an audience and raises questions such as: Where does the scene take place? Who is holding the bomb? What is the person going to do with it? Although the scene starts with a close-up, we still need an establishing shot so the audience does not become confused or disoriented. In figure 4-4, the close-up is followed by a long shot, which answers the questions of who is holding the bomb, and where he is placing it.

figure | 4-4

Storyboard sequence
of a car explosion.

Aesthetic considerations deal with what is pleasing to the eye. A sweeping crane shot of the Paris skyline may appeal aesthetically to a director versus a bird's-eye view of the city. Compositional elements should be explored to maximize the aesthetics of the frame, which will be discussed further in Chapter 5.

Many directors also plan shot selection based on psychological factors. As discussed in Chapter 3, camera framing and camera angles may have an emotional impact on the audience. A viewer may feel more connected to a character, for instance, if close-ups are used. Low-angle shots, on the other hand, may be threatening in certain situations and at other times elevate the character in the shot to a position of power.

One of the most powerful and psychologically frightening scenes is the shower sequence from Hitchcock's *Psycho*. In the scene, Hitchcock creates a montage of quick cuts of Marion Crane taking a shower. There are several subjective close shots in which the audience identifies with Marion as the water cascades down from the showerhead. The subjective shots allow the audience to feel "cleansed" just as Marion. However, midway through the scene we see through the eyes of "Mother," as Norman Bates pulls back the shower curtain and stabs Marion repeatedly. These close shots are taken from various angles, which escalates the audience's own terror.

> *"The last thing you want to do when you are working on a very tight budget is walk on set and say, 'Where does the camera go?'"*
>
> Mark Bristol, Director
> *Natural Selection*

figure | **4-5**

Storyboard from *The Mummy Returns* showing that camera framing and movement may have an emotional impact on the audience.
Courtesy of Universal Studios

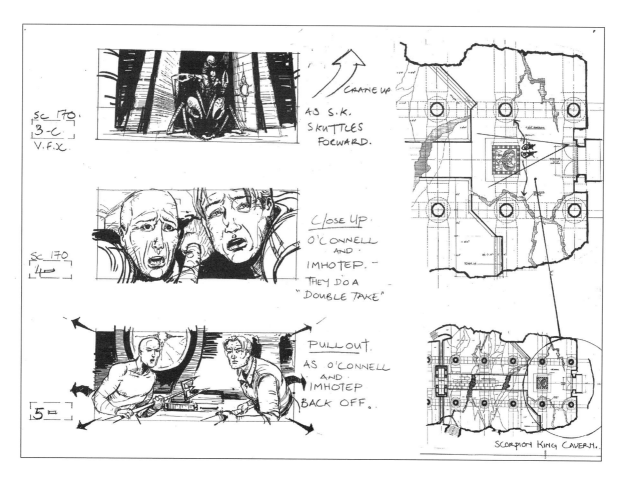

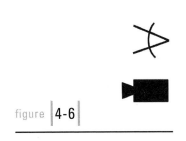

figure **4-6**

Representations of camera icons.

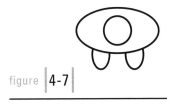

figure **4-7**

Representation of a character icon.

figure **4-8**

Overheads assist in blocking both camera and character movement.

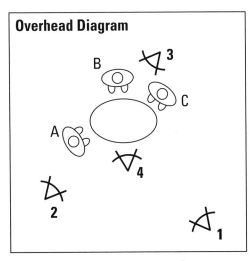

Overhead Diagram

#1: Wide shot of Characters A, B, and C
#2: OTS to Characters B and C
#3: OTS Close-up of Character A
#4: Close-up of Character B

OVERHEAD DIAGRAMMING PROCESS

Think of an overhead diagram (or floor plan) as a map of a location or set. The diagram is an extremely useful tool because it shows both camera placement and character movement within a scene. It also assists the director with identifying potential problems, such as crossing the line of action or not matching eyelines.

Before you diagram a scene, you must first understand the importance of icons, numbering, and how they are used in the planning stages.

Icons

The first step in diagramming the action is to be familiar with the camera and character icons. The camera icon is usually signified as a "V" with a curved line going through it, although you may see it in various other forms, including the shape of a camera.

The character icon is represented in several different ways as well, including a circle that represents an overhead view of a character.

No matter how these icons are visually represented, their job is the same: to communicate the blocking of characters and camera placement within a scene.

Numbering

Each camera position on an overhead diagram is drawn and numbered according to the placement of each shot. If there are multiple cameras used in a scene, each camera needs its own label, such as numbers, letters, or crew positions.

Let's say you have a tracking shot of a car turning the corner (position A) and pulling up into the driveway (position B). This is considered one camera movement. Therefore to differentiate point A from point B, you should assign a subnumber to each key movement. Each camera setup should follow with its own number.

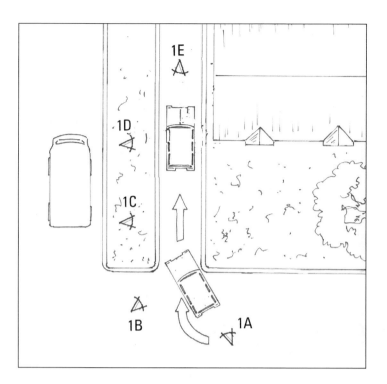

Illustrating Character and Camera Movement

As discussed in Chapter 3, illustrating character or camera movement is difficult on paper. It is not always that easy to tell a pan
from a tracking shot or a zoom from a dolly. Directional arrows,
which indicate movement within the frame, assist the storyboard
artist with clarifying complex objectives. Directional arrows can
be used to show a crane down through city streets, or the simple
motion of a young man throwing pennies into a fountain.

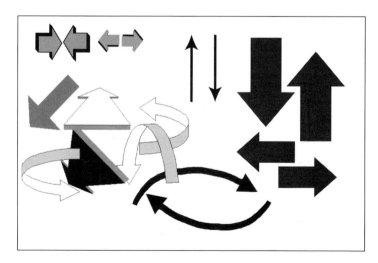

Another technique to illustrate motion within a two-dimensional frame is to expand the storyboard panel into a succession of connected frames. By expanding frame size, the beginning of a shot is illustrated, in addition to where the shot ends. For example, in the film *Touch of Evil*, there is a three-minute crane shot that covers a four-block radius from start to finish. A shot as complex as this would require several key frames to explain to crewmembers what is happening in a scene. Figure 4-11 is an example of manipulating the frame to accommodate various camera moves.

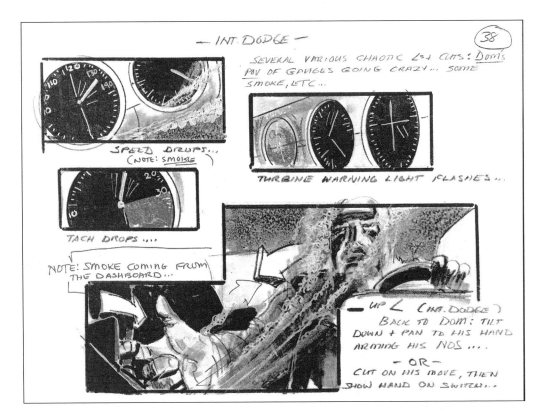

figure | 4-11

Extended frame that showcases the action from *2 Fast 2 Furious.*
Courtesy of Universal Studios

THE STORYBOARD PROCESS

The storyboard is the first visual representation of your story. The process for many artists includes creating thumbnails, roughs, and final storyboards for a project. Although storyboarding process is different for each artist, there is one common thread, and that is to come to a project prepared and organized.

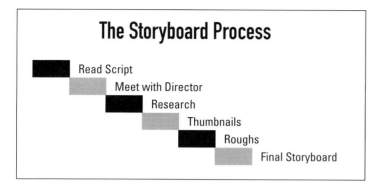

figure | 4-12 |

Steps in the
storyboard process.

Hitchcock's plan for the climactic scene in *North by Northwest* was drawn on a paper place mat.

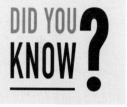

Preparing to Meet with the Director

The first step is to read the finalized script. Many artists create thumbnail sketches in the margins of the script along with written notations before actually meeting with the director. For many, this is an invaluable step because it assists artists with asking questions during the actual meeting with the director. By asking questions, there is less chance for confusion when it actually comes down to storyboarding the project.

A short list of questions to consider as you read the script includes:

- What is the emotional goal of the story?
- What are the personalities of its characters?
- What is the overall mood of the story?
- What is the mood of each scene?
- What colors dominate each scene?
- How do you see the action unfolding?
- What character is in charge of each scene?
- How do you want the audience to feel?

Sometimes you will be asked to create storyboard sketches in conjunction with the screenplay being developed. On many animated productions, the script and storyboards are created concurrently. As a storyboard artist, you will work with the writers, storyboarding gags and visualizing story ideas with quick sketches as the story line develops. However, this is not very common for film productions, which usually finalize the script before the storyboarding phase. We will gain more insight into this process in Chapter 11.

Research

Once you have met with the director, it is time to get to work. Let's say that the director wants you to draw a futuristic landscape. What is the first step you would take?

As a storyboard artist, you will undoubtedly be asked to draw things that are unfamiliar, or hard to call up from memory in accurate detail. Therefore, it is very important to do your homework. Build a catalog or file system of visual references from different categories. But what categories should you include? You will need to acquire slides or pictures of people, vehicles, landscapes, animals, and so forth. Another idea, albeit expensive, is to acquire CD-ROMs of stock photography for reference. A cheaper route is to utilize the Web. There are plenty of free sites on the Web, where you can download photos to build your own digital library. I would also recommend subscribing to magazines to stay current on trends in the marketplace. Another great source is free catalogs such as *Pottery Barn*, *The Electronic Store*, *Crate and Barrel*, car catalogs, and department store catalogs.

One of the best resources for acquiring visual references is at your local library. Libraries offer extensive catalogs to the public, and the services of professional librarians to help you find what you're looking for.

Thumbnails

Creating thumbnails is extremely helpful to the visualization process when a project is first started. They are usually no more than renderings of stick figures or shapes to try out your ideas. As mentioned earlier, thumbnails are also used as a note-taking tool during preproduction meetings. By sketching thumbnails during a meeting, you can brainstorm your ideas, as well as get instant feedback from the director as to whether you are moving in the right direction.

Thumbnails allow you to see what a shot looks like before actually committing the time and effort to fully rendering final storyboards. When creating thumbnails, focus on the overall blocking of a shot to communicate the subject matter, rather than the details.

Roughs

The next step is to create roughs, which are your first full-sized sketches. Images are drawn to proportion and details are carefully broken down regarding what happens in the shot. Roughs block the action, dialogue, and characters in a scene, as well as establish continuity. Once roughs are complete, they are usually presented to the director for approval.

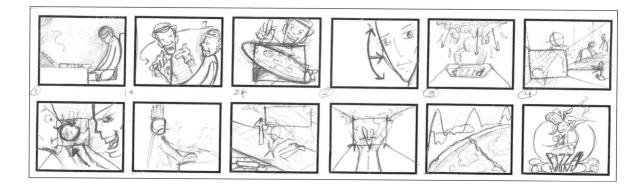

figure 4-13

Thumbnails.

figure 4-14

Rough storyboard from *2 Fast 2 Furious*.
Courtesy of Universal Studios.

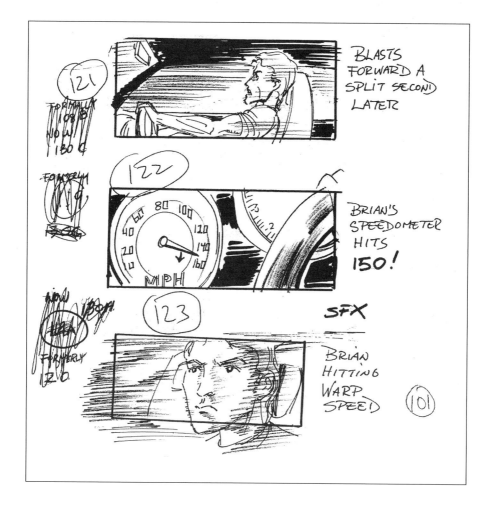

THE STORYBOARD PROCESS

What can you expect while working as a storyboard artist on a film, video game, or animation? The typical work process includes understanding the role of the director and where your skills fit into that process. As a storyboard artist, you must be able to work quickly because of the pressure of deadlines. A typical day may include rendering ten to fifteen highly detailed sketches or thirty to forty rough storyboard panels. You must also understand staging, composition, and editing techniques, as well as be adept at drawing the human figure in motion.

1. Read the script prior to meeting with the director of the project. Come to the meeting prepared with questions.

2. Create thumbnails or take notes while at the meeting regarding how to stage the story. These will come in handy if you have any questions during the meeting or shortly thereafter when you get to work.

3. If necessary, utilize reference and research material to create story sketches.

4. Create rough story sketches that include blocking the action, camera movement, and framing. Sketches should be detailed enough that a director will be able to look at them and understand what is happening in the story.

5. The director reviews the roughs and makes any necessary changes.

6. You must now incorporate the director's comments. This stage may be repeated a few times until the director feels satisfied with the direction of the production.

7. Roughs are now ready to be completed. They should be cleaned up and descriptions should be written neatly or typed under each panel.

8. Submit to director for approval.

Final Boards

Once roughs are approved, they are cleaned up and inked for contrast. Each project has its own guidelines for how final storyboards should be formatted. This may include pencil sketches on 8.5 x 11-inch paper with brief notations describing the camera angle, action, and sound effects of the shot. The number of panels per page varies according to the discretion of the director or artist. Some artists prefer to work with smaller panels (1 x 2-inch panels), whereas others prefer bigger styles such as 3 x 5-inch and 4.5 x 9-inch panels. Smaller panel sizes usually mean you can work quickly, which is an attribute of the storyboard artist since panels are revised often. Within animation, storyboards are often created on index size cards so they can be easily tacked to a bulletin board.

Shot #1 — LS of Bus Interior

Shot #2 — MLS of Crowd

Shot #3 — OTS of Crowd

Shot #4 — ECU of Young Man

figure | 4-15 |

Final storyboard.

When creating final storyboards, you should regard the following guidelines:

- Each panel should adhere to a specific aspect ratio of the production.
- Panels should be numbered according to the corresponding scene in the screenplay. Each panel should also include a shot number.
- Camera angles and action should be described beneath each panel, along with a brief description of the shot and/or any special effects.
- Directional arrows should be used anytime there is significant movement within a panel.

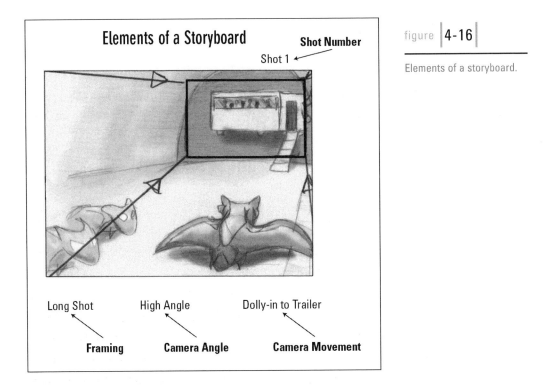

figure | 4-16 |

Elements of a storyboard.

SOME FINAL THOUGHTS

Creating storyboards is a process that involves many different people and quite a bit of research. That is why it is so important to understand the elements that make an effective storyboard. Understanding camera angles, framing, movement, and how they are all put together can be a daunting task. Trust your instincts. Think about the logical flow of a scene as you read the script.

Think about each scene and what it is really about. One of the best ways to learn is to study films. Analyze how directors such as Scorsese, Spielberg, and Fincher put together shots to create meaning. Nowadays, many DVDs include storyboards such as *The Lord of the Rings*, *Spiderman*, and *Spirit*. Studying mediocre films is also helpful to understanding why certain shots may not work. For an extensive list of DVDs featuring storyboards, see Appendix C.

CHAPTER SUMMARY

The first step in the planning process begins with translating the finalized screenplay into a shooting script, which includes a set of instructions for how scenes are broken down into shots. Once the director has the shooting script, a shot list is created, which is a list of the shots intended for each scene. The major elements of the shot list include camera framing, camera angles, and script notations. An overhead diagram is an extremely useful tool because it shows both camera placement and character movement. It also assists with identifying potential problems with blocking a scene. To diagram a scene, you must understand how to number your scenes and use camera and character icons to show character blocking and movement.

When beginning a job, a storyboard artist must have a clear understanding of the script. Asking questions and contributing ideas are useful when meeting with the director. The next step in the creation of storyboards is to create thumbnail drawings, which are extremely loose and usually no more than stick figures. Following thumbnails are the roughs; these are more detailed than thumbnails. Images of the rough are drawn to proportion and show more detail in regard to blocking a scene. The final step is to clean up the boards and ink for contrast. Final storyboards should specify the aspect ratio, panels should be numbered according to the screenplay, and a brief description of the shot type and possibly dialogue should be written under each panel.

in review

1. What is a shooting script?

2. What are the major elements of a shot list?

3. What is the difference between a shot list and an overhead diagram?

4. How are characters and cameras represented within an overhead diagram?

5. Why are camera positions numbered on the overhead diagram?

6. What is the purpose for creating thumbnails?

7. What are several questions that you should ask as you read a script?

8. What happens once the director approves roughs?

9. What are several considerations when creating final storyboards?

10. When should you use directional arrows?

exercises

1. For this exercise, create the shot list, overhead diagram, and storyboard. The scene should average between twelve and fifteen shots.

   A throng of reporters anxiously waits, ready to pounce on the mother and daughter as they pull into their driveway in an old, beat-up station wagon. The mother scans the crowd, in fear as the horde of reporters descends upon the car. The mother leans over her daughter and frantically tries to roll up the passenger window. An aggressive reporter lunges and shoves her microphone into the window opening. The microphone slips out of her grasp into the car, and hits the daughter in the head. The daughter lets out a wail.

2. Split up into teams of two. Each team member will fill the role of director and storyboard artist. The team member who is the "director" will pick an action scene from a screenplay with plenty of movement. (You can download many scripts from the Internet.) The director will discuss with the "storyboard artist" his vision for the scene in question. During the meeting, the storyboard artist should take visual notes by creating thumbnails. Next, the storyboard artist will create quick pencil sketches, based on the director's vision. Once complete, the director will review the roughs, and make revisions, before the storyboard artist moves on to producing the final artwork. These storyboards should include shot descriptions beneath each panel and be numbered accordingly. When complete, team members should switch roles.

| composition |

objectives

Learn how the elements of design affect shot arrangement

Express the mood and intent of a story line with two-dimensional images

Understand the emotional and psychological impact of geometric forms and lines

Apply the rule of thirds to storyboard panels

introduction

As moviegoers, we expect to be entertained for two hours by both the story and the visuals for the price of admission. Sometimes we can overlook technical problems, such as a poorly lit scene or flat composition, if the story is really strong. It is the message that is the most important element in a scene, but if technical problems become too apparent, it will ultimately weaken the message, no matter how engaging the story line.

Visual style begins and ends with the composition, which in film, television, and animation is the arrangement of elements such as line, weight, and shape within a two-dimensional frame shape. To create a visually strong composition, you need to know the purpose for each shot in a scene, and how that shot relates to the overall production. Once you have an idea of what you want to suggest with a shot, you can arrange the elements of the composition to give it meaning.

Suppose two characters are about to say their wedding vows. What can you imply about the characters or the situation? Maybe the script calls for the characters to appear radiant and excited. Or perhaps you need to convey their uneasiness in the composition because the couple has made the wrong decision. Elements of the composition can be arranged in a distinct order to evoke a specific response, whether it is joy, fear, angst, or any other emotion.

This chapter explores the visual components of composition, and how those elements are balanced in a two-dimensional frame to give it meaning.

figure | 5-1 |

Elements of a composition are arranged to evoke a specific emotional response.
Courtesy of Dorian Soto

COMPOSITION

figure | 5-2 |

Line as an element of design.

VISUAL STYLE

Before a production begins, every film and animation director, game designer, and art director needs to establish the objectives for a project. It is critical that the director or designer of a project has a good eye for how to plan the overall visual style of a project down to the purpose for each shot within a frame. Director John Woo (*Face/Off*), for instance, plans each of his films as if he were creating a poem or a painting.

Today's directors and designers must depict emotion and mood through how the elements of a shot are arranged to further the message of the production.

THE VISUAL ELEMENTS

The elements of visual design include line, shape, value, texture, and color. Together they form a composition. Sometimes the most stunning scenes break the rules of composition. However, before you break the rules, you must first understand how design elements communicate meaning and ideas.

The arrangement of visual elements evokes specific emotional responses from audiences. For example, a diagonal line implies a different meaning than a horizontal line; the color green means something different than red. It is important that artists consider the psychological and emotional impact they want to achieve with the arrangement of such elements. If there are too many elements within an image, for instance, a composition becomes distracting. Any distraction will destroy the viewer's fragile suspension of disbelief, leaving them confused or even irritated. When sketching storyboards, all the elements of an image need to be considered for emotional impact, including where the audience should focus their attention.

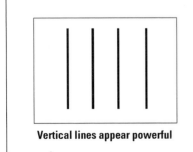

Vertical lines appear powerful

Horizontal lines imply stability

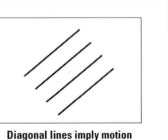

Diagonal lines imply motion

Lines

The most basic element of design is the line; it can be horizontal, vertical, curved, bold, implied, or diagonal. Lines can be roads, fences, body motion, or an endless list of objects. They can lead the eye, evoke movement, or divide a space into separate units. Lines can also create a sense of depth within an image, as in figure 5-3.

figure | 5-3 |

Lines lead the eye into the image.
© Caz Russo

A frame's composition may be expressed with any combination of lines in relationship to one another. Our eyes tend to travel along these lines, moving from one part of a frame to another, which gives the composition meaning. If your message is one of graveness or urgency, the use of straight lines in the frame will help convey that message. One of *Psycho's* beautifully composed scenes is when Norman and Marion have sandwiches in the study. Hitchcock frames the character of Norman Bates with harsh vertical and diagonal lines. The light that cuts across Norman's face is angular and quite dramatic, which suggests his sinister side. The heavy lines of the picture frames, candelabra, and chest within the frame also add to portraying his darker side, which is contrasted quite effectively by the curves of his victim Marion.

Horizontal and Vertical Lines

Horizontal lines follow from left to right, or side to side. Horizontal lines may suggest stability, quietness, or restfulness. Many western films use strong horizontal lines to communicate the vastness of a landscape.

| **TIP** |

Incorporate sharp shapes and lines in your composition to imply motion and tension.

figure | 5-4 |

Horizontal and vertical lines.

Vertical lines, on the other hand, run from top to bottom, or up and down. These lines are stronger and more active than horizontal lines and often take visual precedence over any other lines in the frame. For example, a cactus in a landscape would attract the viewer's attention because of its vertical elements.

Diagonal Lines

Diagonal lines are straight lines that appear to move because they are drawn from corner to corner. Objects that are arranged in a diagonal composition appear to move even if the object is static. Diagonal lines may suggest action, violence, or energy. They may also convey a character that is unstable, or make the viewer feel tense and uncomfortable.

figure | 5-5 |

Diagonal lines convey a feeling of excitement and action within the image.

Courtesy of Jamie McCullough

Curved Lines

Curved lines have different meaning, depending on their shape. Sharp curves, such as ocean waves, suggest turbulence. Soft curves, on the other hand, imply a sensual or soothing quality, and suggest harmony. Another curve-shaped line is the S-curve, which is considered fluid and graceful. The S-curve can be the main subject of a composition or can be used as a framing element or leading line. A popular use of the S-curve is the curve of a stream through trees.

| TIP |

Curved lines tend to slow down the action, and should be avoided for high impact scenes.

figure | 5-6 |

The curve of the road leads the viewer into the image.

Courtesy of J. Allen McFadden

Jagged Lines

Jagged lines are a combination of multiple lines, such as horizontal and vertical, or diagonal and curved lines. Lines that are jagged tend to convey a sense of restlessness and aggressiveness. A bolt of lightning illuminating the sky is the most basic jagged line.

figure | 5-7 |

Jagged lines convey a sense of restlessness or perhaps aggressiveness.

Courtesy of Jamie McCullough

SCENE SHOT:14-HAS from above cab looking down a ramp that ends at an iron gate overlooking a huge glowing chasm.

Shapes and Forms

Shapes are outlines of objects that are defined by their height and width. These objects tend to lack mass and often appear as silhouettes, which are dark outlines of subjects or objects with no detail.

The three basic shapes are the square, circle, and triangle. Shapes are often grouped together to create meaning within a frame. Each of these shapes has psychological values associated with it. The square, for example, is associated with honesty, order, equality, and rigidity. A triangle is often conveyed as dynamic and enterprising, and the circle gives the feeling of safety and protection.

When shapes acquire the third dimension of depth, they morph into forms. For example, a circle is a shape, whereas a sphere is a form.

| NOTE |

To emphasize a shape, place the subject or object on a background of an opposing color or surround it with contrasting shapes.

figure | 5-8 |

Objects that lack mass tend to appear as silhouettes.

Courtesy of Mr. Rod

The Triangular Composition

The triangle is one of the most common shapes used to frame people and objects. In a triangular composition, our eye travels around the triangle's three separate points in dynamic motion. The person at the height of the apex appears superior, when framing groups of people in a triangle composition. If the triangle is reversed, and the apex is at the bottom, the person often appears weaker.

Actual triangles may also be abstract by positioning three subsidiary points of interest to form a frame for your point of interest.

"The audience is always looking through slats of a fence or past the curtain of a fogged-up window that looks out into the snow, so you have layer upon layer upon layer within the image. There's always something between us and the subject."

Scott Hicks, Director
Snow Falling on Cedars

Circular and Arch Compositions

The second most common composition is circular, which often symbolizes harmony. A circular composition draws the viewer and the subject of the frame together in an intimate image. In the film *ET*, Spielberg uses circles as a motif from the wheels of the children's bicycles to the moon, to the circular gates of the spacecraft.

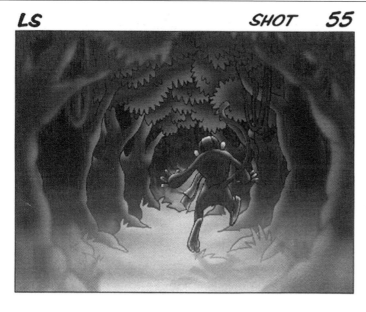

LS   SHOT   55

LUCID FOLLOWS AFTER MASLOW

The appearance of arches is another compositional element that can lead the eye, in addition to acting as a framing element. A film that is rife with both arch and circular framing is the classic film *Casablanca*. Many of the characters were blocked in the foreground of Moorish archways, which extend beyond a semicircle and provide an airy effect to a shot.

figure **5-11**

Arches can lead the eye or provide a feeling of spaciousness to an image.
Courtesy of Jamie McCullough

Overlap

Overlapping objects not only affects depth of field, but also creates a pleasing composition. To create objects that overlap in a sketch, all you need to do is draw the objects closer together. For example, let's say you have four characters that appear next to each other; this makes for a flat composition. But if you stagger the individuals with each one slightly in front of the next, this makes for a much more interesting image.

figure **5-12**

By staggering the four characters in this image, depth is added to the frame.

Contrast and Similarity

Our eye is drawn to contrasts in shape, weight, color, and size. The differences in weight or color will draw our attention to the dominant object. If you placed the Pillsbury Dough Boy, for instance, against a dark background, there would be significant contrast between the white of the Dough Boy and the blackness of the background. However, if two objects of similar color or size are next to one another, the contrast will be less intense. In a scene from the film *The Godfather*, Don Corleone holds a rose in his hand. The rose draws the audience's attention away from Don Corleone because of its warm color and its placement in the frame.

figure 5-13

This image illustrates high-
and low-tonal contrast.

Organizing elements by size is also commonplace in visual design. Objects of the same size may be grouped together, such as with crowd scenes. In such instances, we take in the composition as a whole. Size may also have the opposite effect by isolating an object of the same size from the group. A general who addresses the troops, for instance, or leads the charge in battle, is isolated from the masses. In such situations, our eye is first attracted to the isolated character or object.

figure 5-14

Objects of similar size are
seen as a whole.
Courtesy of Dorian Soto

figure 5-15

Our eye is attracted to isolated
objects of similar size.
Courtesy of Todd Ries

Texture

All surfaces have texture. There is texture you can touch, such as the fabric of a coat, and texture that is an illusion to the human eye. Texture may mean the grain or saturation of a film stock, but it can also be implied in film. Visual texture adds a richness to a shot that otherwise might be missing. Director Ridley Scott gave *Blade Runner* a dark, visual texture that became the standard for later films in the genre. There are several different types of textures that can be represented in your drawings. Two of the most popular are smooth and rough.

figure | 5-16 |

Texture brings out the details of this image.
© Jean-Christophe Hyacinthe

"I found some marvelous locations in New York—in Harlem poolrooms. I saw marvelous colors and textures in these old, run-down places, and I thought that the film was a film of texture, really. To me it was a texture of people who are really rotting away, a decadent story."

Bob Rossen, Director
The Hustler

Smooth

Smooth textures are seen on a shiny saxophone, a chrome bumper, and skin tones. When a surface is smooth, it is devoid of any roughness. Smooth textures such as glass reflect light. When drawing smooth textures, you want to show the irregular shapes by capturing the contrasts and bringing out the highlights that are reflected in the surface.

Rough

Rough textures are visible to the eye. They sometimes appear jagged or irregular. Textures that are rough include weaved baskets, the bark of a tree, or a burlap sack.

figure |5-17|

Texture can be implied, such as an image of a snowy mountaintop.
© Jean-Christophe Hyacinthe

Patterns

Patterns occur when lines, shapes, texture, or colors are repeated. Seating in a football stadium creates a visual pattern, as do tree branches.

For a pattern to be established, there must be repetition of the elements. Repeating patterns tend to grab our attention and are extremely powerful in making a visual statement. However, if a pattern is static, it tends to be boring. For example, a shot of a hallway that has a dozen doors that are all the same size and color is uninteresting. But if you combine patterns with a number of other elements, the composition will form a powerful image that establishes both the mood and theme of a production.

figure |5-18|

Repeating patterns grab our attention.
Courtesy of Todd Ries

Positive and Negative Space

There are positive forms of objects and negative spaces that surround these objects. When you pick up a pencil to draw, the objects that you create are converted into positive and negative space. Often, negative spaces are regarded as passive in contrast to positive space. Negative space does not mean it should be labeled as the background. In many motion pictures, the negative space of the image is just as important as the objects that make up the frame. Although objects are separate from the background, they both work together to create an interesting composition.

Positive space is masked in black, while in the second frame the negative space is masked in black.

Remember, each time that you draw an object, you are creating a negative space as well. The most notable illustration of positive and negative space is the vase shape that disappears when you notice the two profiles. This illusion is created when there is indecision.

When creating a dynamic composition, you do not want the objects and the backgrounds to compete with one another. By emphasizing an object's color, size, texture, etc., you can accentuate that which is the primary focus in the frame.

FRAMING, MOVEMENT, AND MEANING

Unlike a typical frame, the border of the film frame is part of the shot. Artists create not only the illusion of movement within the frame by the placement of characters and objects, but also meaning. For instance, an ascending vertical movement such as several graduates throwing their caps in the air suggests growth. Objects that descend have the opposite effect. A piano, for instance, that falls on the head of Wile E. Coyote suggests danger and heaviness.

figure | 5-20 |

The wide angle lens provides the illusion of movement.
Courtesy of Mr. Rod

Characters can enter or exit a frame from the right or left, or from the top or bottom. Characters or objects moving from left to right usually feels more natural and engaging to the eye than right to left movement. Framing objects at the top of the frame often carries more psychological weight than if a character is composed at the bottom of the screen; that is because the top carries more power and influence than the bottom.

A well-framed shot takes into consideration not only what goes into the frame, but what is excluded from it as well. Framing only a character's feet walking down a dark corridor, for instance, creates suspense and viewer interest—more so than if we saw the entire person.

When composing the elements, shot composition should generally have only one main center of interest. Even if a shot takes place in a crowded subway, you want nothing within that composition to upstage the main point of interest, especially when the viewer has only a few seconds to comprehend the meaning before it changes.

Framing an object toward one of the four corners of the frame creates tension, which produces a visually stimulating image. If we were to compare the right and left sides of the frame, the right side often carries more weight than the left. Oftentimes, unsavory characters are framed on the right side, which creates more tension and weight than if framed on the left.

figure | 5-23 |

The right carries more weight than the left.

figure | 5-24 |

Which of the two compositions is more dynamic? Changing the framing and angling the character makes for a much more exciting composition.

Frame: 1

Frame: 2

Objects that are framed in the center lack the same compositional weight as objects nearer to one of the corners. That is why when framing your point of interest, whether it is a person, setting, or object, you want to try to avoid centered placement. Compositions that are centered are usually flat and uninteresting unless it is used as a visual motif. Think of it this way: if you have a seesaw and an object is placed in the middle, nothing will happen. But if you place an object on the left or right side of the seesaw, the object will appear to tip toward that side. This will cause the object to tumble visually.

Closed Frame

Movie screens, computer monitors, and television sets all have screens that are confined by borders. The lines of the border or frame tell us where the action stops. For example, if the person opening a refrigerator door is shown within the frame, it is considered a complete action that provides all the pertinent information necessary for the audience to comprehend. There is nothing left to the imagination because the frame lines automatically lock the picture.

figure | 5-25 |

The subject appears enclosed in the frame.

Open Frame

An open frame requires some thinking on the part of the audience. This type of framing often suggests choice. With an open frame, not every action is laid out inside the frame. Rather, the action moves in and out of the frame. The audience assumes that something is happening beyond the frame. To create an open frame, there needs to be movement that is visually more powerful than the frame itself. A classic example of an open space is the ship that travels at light speed through the galaxy as the stars stretch to infinity. What if we establish a scene where a character is watching television? If the character reaches for the remote off screen, we do not need to show it as an insert shot. In open framing, the audience assumes that there is something beyond the frame, such as a remote.

figure | 5-26 |

The motion of the character appears to extend beyond the frame as she moves right, and the car appears to move left.

Rule of Thirds

The simplest method to employ when composing a dynamic frame is the rule of thirds. To exercise the rule of thirds, divide your image into three equal sections, vertically and horizontally. Generally, a pleasing composition is achieved by placing objects near one of the four cross points. The horizon lines should be in either the upper third or the lower third of the frame. Vertical lines should be placed one-third or two-thirds of the way across the frame. Dynamic impact is achieved by placing objects on one of the points of interest.

The Center of Interest

What if you have various two shot, triangular, and circular compositions that feature several players in a frame at one time? In such compositions, there should be only one center of interest. You do not want two characters or objects in a triangular composition competing for the spotlight. Instead, you want to attract the audience's attention to one point. For instance, if you have several people seated at a dinner table and you have most of the characters look at one particular person, you create a center of interest. Also, if you have an individual and an object within the frame, have the person look at the object.

Headroom

When framing a subject, you must consider headroom, which refers to the amount of space between the top of the head and the frame. If there is too much space, the subject will appear short. If there is not enough headroom, the subject will appear crowded. A technique for achieving adequate headroom is to align the eyes of your character to the top one-third line.

| TIP |

When you want the audience's attention to be directed to the ground, place the horizon on the upper one-third line of the composition.

figure | 5-27 |

Placing objects near the four points creates a more interesting composition.

Appropriate headroom

Too much headroom

Too little headroom

Lead room

Lead room, also called look space, refers to the amount of space that is in front of the character to the edge of the frame. Generally, you want about two-thirds lead room in front of a character. This allows the audience to comprehend where the character is moving (or looking), which produces an aesthetically pleasing image.

figure | 5-28 |

Headroom is the amount of space between the top of the head and the top of the frame.

The amount of lead room not only affects aesthetics, it also affects mood. For example, if a character is placed at the edge of the frame with no lead space, it creates an uncomfortable and tense image. Often the framing implies that a character has a negative outlook on life because they have nowhere to look or move.

figure | 5-29 |

Lead room is the amount of space in front of a character.

figure 5-30

No look space creates a tense
and uncomfortable image.

TYPES OF BALANCE

Balance compares the right and left side of a composition according to its visual weight and importance. For instance, if you divide an image in half and the elements on each side are equal, the composition is symmetrically balanced. There are several factors that work in combination that contribute to the balance of a composition. These factors may include position, color, proportion, or direction of the elements.

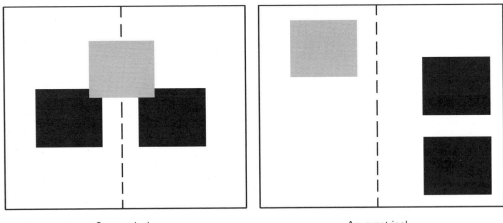

Symmetrical   Asymmetrical

figure 5-31

A comparison of symmetrical and
asymmetrical balance.

Symmetrical Balance

A symmetrically balanced image pulls the eye away from the edges, to the center of the frame. Characters or objects in a symmetrically balanced shot are almost always framed straight on with no camera angling. The two shot, for instance, is an example of a symmetrically balanced frame with one character positioned on one side of the frame, and another character repeated on the opposite side.

Symmetrical balance usually favors tranquility, but may also imply conflict or confinement. Director Sam Mendes used symmetrical balance in *American Beauty* to reinforce family relationships that were often claustrophobic and rigid. By placing his characters in the middle of the frame, Mendes created a sense of imprisonment and austerity.

Looking at a storyboard panel, symmetrical balance is achieved by dividing the frame down the middle, or across the middle. All the objects on one side of the screen are mirrored on the other side. These elements are identical or similar in terms of the number of objects, colors, or other elements.

Another type of symmetrical balance is radial symmetry. Radial symmetry radiates from a central focal point in a square composition. All the elements lead your eye toward the center.

figure | 5-32 |

Symmetrical balance is when one side is the mirror image of the other side.

Asymmetrical Balance

An asymmetrical composition is achieved when both sides of a frame are similar in visual weight, but are very different in appearance. In an asymmetrical composition, the two sides of the frame may differ in shape, value, position, texture, and color. For instance, our eyes are drawn to vibrant colors. In an asymmetrical composition, smaller areas of colors on one side of a frame may contrast with larger areas of more muted colors on the other side. Such framing has more energy and tension than a symmetrical composition.

figure | 5-33 |

The sides in an asymmetrical composition are not identical, but vary in weight.

In an asymmetrical composition, the dominant object or figure should not be placed on the same horizon line with opposing or weaker elements; it should go above or below the horizon to attract the attention of the viewer. A triangular composition is often used to reinforce asymmetrical balance. In such cases, the main figure is placed to one side of the frame, at the bottom or top of the apex, to achieve the desired effect.

Unbalanced Composition

An unbalanced frame has no unity in theme or weight. It seems as if objects within the composition might actually tip over. A canted angle places characters off balance, which creates a feeling of tension. For instance, a psychotic serial killer shot from a skewed angle implies his derangement. Unbalanced compositions may be used in films that want to convey fear, violence, or visual interest.

CHAPTER SUMMARY

An image is an extremely complex phenomenon. Factors such as line, shape, form, texture, and scale all work together to create meaning in a composition. Psychological and emotional values also affect composition and the arrangement of elements. Diagonal lines may make viewers feel uncomfortable and tense. Circles imply balance and harmony.

The center of interest is another component of a well-framed shot. When composing the frame, you want nothing to detract from the center of interest. In such compositions, you want to attract the viewer's attention to one point within the image. The rule of thirds is one method for composing a dynamic frame with a strong center of interest. You must also consider both headroom and lead room. Headroom refers to the distance between the top of the subject's head and the top of the frame. Lead room is based on the amount of "look space" a character has within the frame; too little look space will make the viewer feel claustrophobic.

Many two shots are symmetrically balanced. The elements in these shots are similar in terms of the number of objects, colors, or other elements. Asymmetrical compositions are more dynamic than symmetrical shots since characters or objects of asymmetrical compositions vary in visual weight.

in review

1. How do lines affect composition?

2. Psychological responses are attached to the direction of a line. List three responses for diagonal, vertical, and horizontal lines.

3. There are multiple points of attraction in an image. What makes the audience attracted to these areas?

4. *E.T.* represents an example of a circular motif. Explain.

5. What type of shots are associated with symmetry and asymmetry?

6. When would a composition be considered unbalanced?

7. How would you apply the rule of thirds to a composition?

exercises

1. Select a scene from a film or video and compile a shot-by-shot analysis, which includes a description of the design elements for each shot. Shot composition should also describe camera and subject movement. The analysis should describe how the arrangement of elements contributes to the impact of the shot or scene.

2. Create a storyboard for one of the following scenes. The story should fall within a range of fifteen to twenty shots. Develop this idea according to the guidelines of the rule of thirds.

   Every afternoon at precisely four o'clock p.m. a woman sits in the back corner of a café, sipping a skim mocha latte.

   - The woman is escaping the stress of three kids, a dog, and an unemployed husband.

   - The woman is secretly in love with the café owner.

   - The woman is a secret agent, sent to spy on the establishment across the street.

| perspective |

objectives

introduction

We see the world in three dimensions, but when that world is recorded onto film or video, depth becomes an illusion. The concept of perspective is based on the way the human eye sees the world. Our eyes are constantly in motion, scanning objects and the environment. We view the world from different positions that alter the way objects appear. If we look out the window from the sixth floor of an apartment complex, for instance, the environment looks much different than if we were on the ground looking up.

So, what happens when you want to convey a feeling of depth, but the material you are working with is essentially flat, and two-dimensional? As a storyboard artist, you need to have a firm grasp on the laws of visual perspective to make objects appear to have dimension and distance. Understanding perspective allows you to consider different viewpoints of a shot.

The most regarded system of representation is linear perspective. Critical to linear perspective is lens choice, and the distance between the camera and the subject. Perspective will change anytime the lens or camera position is rearranged. Other important cues include overlapping, texture, spacing, size, and foreshortening.

This chapter will familiarize you with the terms and principles behind these basic concepts and how they contribute to the creation of dynamic storyboards.

PERSPECTIVE

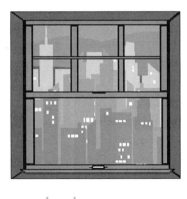

figure | 6-1 |

The picture plane is similar to an imaginary window that we view a scene through.

PICTURE PLANE

The picture plane is similar to an actual window. As we look out a window, we can draw exactly what we see on its surface. In order to view an object, you must direct your gaze in the direction of the object in question, which is referred to as the line of sight or eye line. If our eye line shifts, the window needs to shift as well, otherwise the scene outside will move out of alignment. That is because the imaginary picture plane follows our every move. It moves wherever our eyes move. For instance, if we shift our line of sight up or down, the picture plane also tilts up or down. If we look left or right, so will the picture plane. As you plan your storyboards, think of your drawing paper as the picture plane through which you view locations and objects from different vantage points.

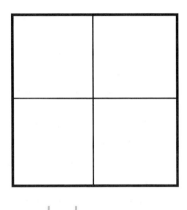

figure | 6-2 |

Which quadrant of the picture plane do you look at first?

THE HORIZON LINE AND THE VANISHING POINT

Standing at the foot of the shore looking out toward the ocean, it appears that the ocean meets the sky. This is called the horizon, which is the same as the horizon line, an imaginary line that is always at our eye level. An object's relationship with the horizon line shows whether it is a low-angle, high-angle, or normal view.

figure | 6-3 |

The horizon line is always at our eye level.

Courtesy of Jean-Christophe Hyacinthe

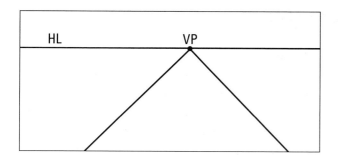

figure | 6-4a |

The horizon line and vanishing point.

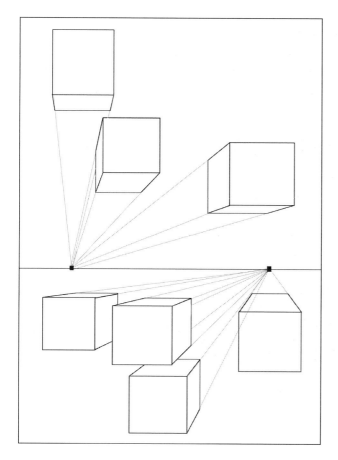

figure | 6-4b |

To create the illusion that we are looking up, draw the object above the horizon, and to create the illusion that we are looking down, draw it below the horizon line.

The vanishing point is a point on the horizon line where the parallel lines of an object recede to the horizon. Objects that are parallel to one another have the same vanishing point. Objects that are at different angles have their own vanishing point.

The simplest method for understanding the relationship between the horizon and the vanishing point is to imagine standing between two train tracks. When you look toward the horizon, it appears that the parallel tracks actually converge at a point in the distance.

figure | 6-5 |

The convergence lines in both drawings move away from the viewer and converge at the vanishing point.

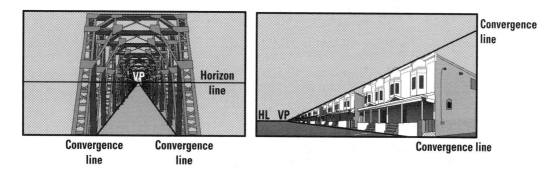

figure | 6-6 |

The lines of the road appear to converge in the distance.
Courtesy of Jean-Christophe Hyacinthe

One-Point Perspective

One-point perspective is the most common system used to render three-dimensional objects and environments on two-dimensional surfaces. In one-point perspective, there is only one vanishing point. For instance, if you look down a road, the lines of the road appear to recede to a single vanishing point on the horizon. There are three types of lines used in one-point perspective: vertical lines, horizontal lines, and orthogonal lines.

Vertical lines are perpendicular to the horizon line and the bottom of your panel. Horizontal lines go from left to right and are parallel to the bottom edge of a panel. Orthogonal lines are parallel lines that recede to the vanishing point. Remember our road? The outside edges of the road are examples of orthogonal lines. Objects that contain parallel lines may be drawn in one-point perspective, such as room interiors, tables, and chairs.

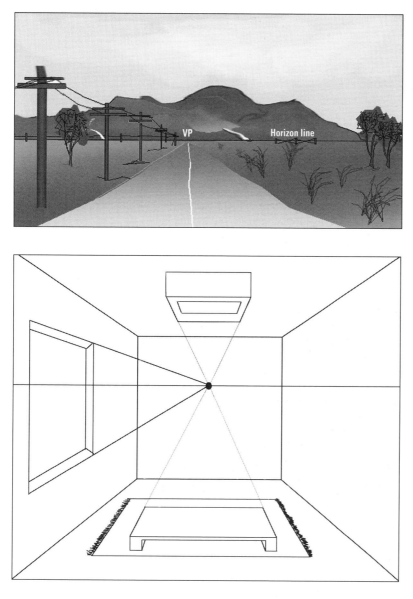

figure | 6-7a |

One-point perspective.

figure | 6-7b |

Interior of room being drawn in one-point perspective.

| NOTE |

Flip through your favorite magazines and select several pictures. Try to locate the vanishing point for objects by extending the lines that are parallel.

Two-Point Perspective

Applying two-point perspective to your storyboard will help you to draw environments and objects from different angles. Shots drawn in two-point perspective open up the image so the viewer does not have to look at a wall from straight on or down a passageway to a single point. That is because two-point perspective has two vanishing points—one to the right and one to the left on the horizon line.

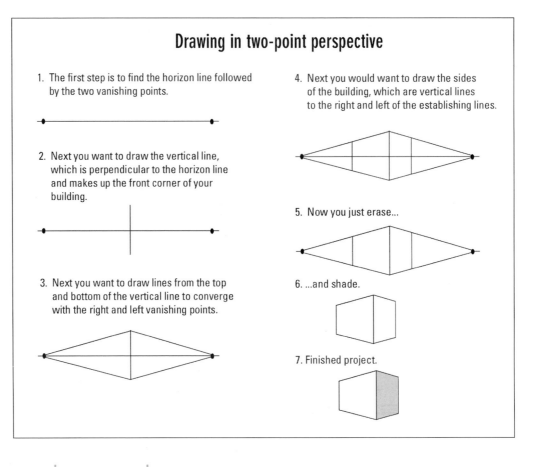

Drawing in two-point perspective

1. The first step is to find the horizon line followed by the two vanishing points.

2. Next you want to draw the vertical line, which is perpendicular to the horizon line and makes up the front corner of your building.

3. Next you want to draw lines from the top and bottom of the vertical line to converge with the right and left vanishing points.

4. Next you would want to draw the sides of the building, which are vertical lines to the right and left of the establishing lines.

5. Now you just erase...

6. ...and shade.

7. Finished project.

figures **6-8a** and **6-8b**

Two-point perspective.

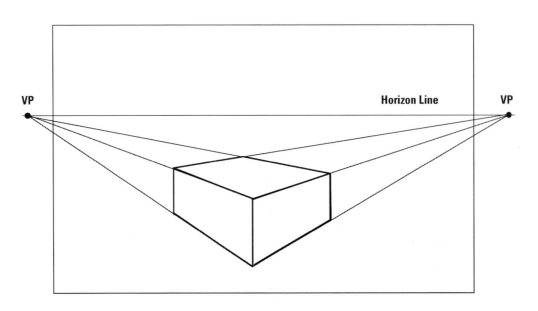

VP   Horizon Line   VP

There are three sets of lines in two-point perspective drawings: a set of lines that converge on the left at a vanishing point, a set of lines that converge on the right at a vanishing point, and vertical lines. These lines form a square corner. If the locations of the vanishing points change, the angle of the object may change, which causes a change in the object's appearance.

figure | 6-8c |

Two-point perspective.

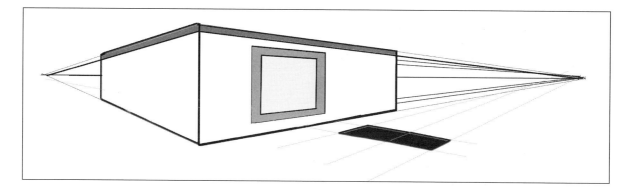

Three-Point Perspective

Three-point perspective drawings typically involve viewers looking up or down at a scene. All lines in three-point perspective drawings recede to one of three vanishing points. Two of these vanishing points rest somewhere on the horizon line, while the third is set either well below, or above, the eye line. The vanishing point that is above the horizon line gives the impression of a low-angle view. When observing a building from this low angle, it is necessary to tilt the picture plane upward. When the vanishing point is below the horizon line, it creates the illusion of a bird's-eye view. Viewers tend to feel farther away from what they are looking at if it is a bird's-eye view.

| TIP |

Place the vanishing points far from each other on the horizon, otherwise your object will appear to have a warped perspective.

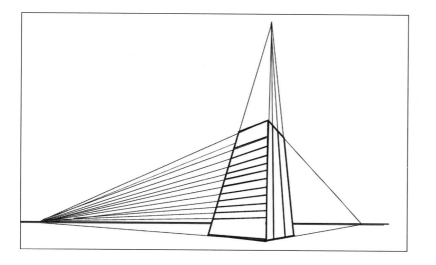

figure | 6-9 |

Three-point perspective.

figure | 6-10 |

Three-point perspective.

Atmospheric Perspective

Observing objects in the distance is often difficult because of particles in the air, such as dust and moisture. Objects that are farther away tend to be a little "hazier" and sometimes cast a bluish tint. To achieve this effect in storyboard panels, color saturation is decreased and background objects are blurred. This gives the impression of depth when contrasted with objects in the foreground.

figure | 6-11 |

Atmospheric perspective causes the image to lose detail and focus.

The Lord of the Rings: The Twin Towers is rife with shots of atmospheric perspective as Frodo and Sam cross the Dead Marshes on their journey. According to Director of Photography Andrew Lesnie, "Anyone who walks through the Dead Marshes is prone to fall under the influence of the trapped souls, which Frodo does briefly. We therefore depicted the Marshes as a misty, unnatural environment, with sunlight weakened by the atmosphere."

Foreshortening

Foreshortening is the process of applying perspective to objects and figures. When you foreshorten an object, you make one part appear closer to you than the other parts. Let's say you have a long pipe lying on its side. As the pipe turns toward you, we see less of its sides until ultimately the only part visible is the circle of the top of the pipe. For example, if you are drawing a bird's-eye view of a building, you will see less of its sides than if you drew a low-angle shot.

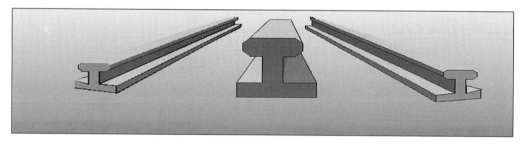

figure | **6-12a**

The lines appear shorter in order to provide the illusion of depth.

figure | **6-12b**

Foreshortened view.

Foreshortening tricks the eye into giving the viewer the illusion of depth. Simple objects such as books, rulers, ladders, and so forth are relatively easy to draw as foreshortened. However, more complex shapes, such as the human figure and animals, are more difficult to reconstruct on paper. When drawing such objects, you must train your eye to see three-dimensional objects in 2D.

Overlap

Overlapping objects creates the illusion of space. When one object is placed over a second object, the first object appears closer than the second one. This rule applies across any distance, and contributes to the illusion of depth. For example, the sun appears smaller when it sets behind the mountains. When blocking a shot, you should overlap characters and objects to create depth.

figure | 6-13 |

By partially overlapping images, you create depth within the image.

Texture Gradient

Most surfaces, such as walls, buildings, fields, and roads, have a texture. The closer the object is, the more detail we can see. As the surface gets farther away from us, the texture gets finer and appears smoother.

Circles in Perspective

Automobiles, tables, plates, lamps, and many other objects are made up of circles. To create three-dimensional objects, the rules of perspective must apply. Circles or ellipses that are near the horizon line are seen straight on and are drawn as straight lines, while ellipses farther from the horizon are drawn bigger.

figures **6-14a** and **6-14b**

Many objects are made up of circles, including a car's steering wheel and the cylinder of a gun.

Top: Courtesy of Jamie McCullough

Bottom: Courtesy of Henry Alfonzo

The best method to draw a circle in perspective is to draw it inside a square, in perspective. The circle is intersected with two axis lines, which creates four quadrants. The point where the two lines cross within the circle creates a T. Whether you are drawing a perfectly round circle or an elongated circle, the relationship of the two lines stays the same. The diagonal lines assist in finding the position of each arc of the circle.

figure | 6-15 |

Circles in perspective.

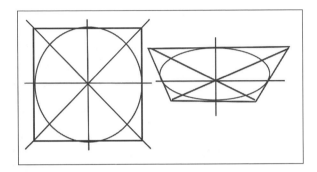

Size Perspective

When flying in an airplane, everything on the ground appears to be miniature. The illusion of small houses, swimming pools, and cars speckle the ground. If we put our hand to the window, we can cover whole neighborhoods with our palm. Obviously, we know that houses on the ground are much bigger than our hand, but the farther away objects are from our viewpoint, the smaller they appear. A size relationship is made of all familiar objects. When subjects of familiar size are included, they help to establish the scale of a picture or drawing. Scale helps the viewer determine the actual size or relative size of the objects in the picture.

figure | 6-16 |

Dwindling size perspective.

Relative Motion

Relative motion is a considerable depth cue to consider for movies, television, and animation. The camera captures the relative motion of objects, which contributes to the overall depth of a scene. Whenever we move, images located at different distances seem to move at different speeds. Close objects seem to move quicker than objects that are farther away, such as distant mountain ranges. Also objects that are closer appear to move in the opposite direction to our own movement, whereas objects farther away appear to move in the same direction.

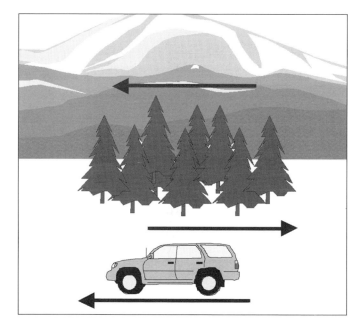

figure |6-17|

Objects that are close appear to move in the opposite direction, whereas objects that are farther away move slower and appear to move in the same direction. Extremely distant objects appear not to move at all.

figure |6-18|

Shallow depth of field.
© Jean-Christophe Hyacinthe

DEPTH OF FIELD

Depth of field, which refers to how much of the frame is in focus, both in front and behind an object, is another effect used to create depth in your images. If you were to view a long road that is aligned with telephone poles, for example, the poles in the distance look smaller than those close to you. If you focus your attention on the telephone poles that are close to you, the ones in the distance will appear out of focus. This effect is often used in film and animation to direct the audience's attention to certain details within the shot.

For instance, if your focus is on a character in the foreground and the background is out of focus, this is considered shallow depth of field. In such situations, our eyes tend to naturally go to the object or individual that is in focus.

If both the foreground and background are in focus, this is considered wide depth of field.

Orson Welles and cinematographer Greg Toland popularized a technique called deep focus cinematography in the classic film *Citizen Kane*. Deep focus refers to a strategy that keeps the foreground, middle ground, and background in focus, giving each plane equal importance.

figure **6-19a** and **6-19b**

Wide depth of field. The foreground and the background are in focus.
© Jean-Christophe Hyacinthe

Wide lens

Normal lens

Telephoto lens

figure **6-20**

Different lens types.

Depth is also created through lens type, and the amount that a lens is opened to let in light, also known as aperture. If the aperture for a lens is small, less light is let in, which results in a greater depth of field. A wider aperture lets in more light, which results in a shallow depth of field.

Lenses

Camera lenses play an indispensable role in determining depth of field within an image. The three main lenses are the wide-angle, normal, and telephoto lens. Each of these lenses tells a story quite differently. In his book *Making Movies*, Sidney Lumet uses an example from the film *Murder on the Orient Express* to illustrate the power of the lens.

In the film, the director uses various lenses to tell the story. During the body of the picture, various scenes take place, which were retold at the end of the movie by Hercule Poirot, the genius detective. While he described the incidents, the scenes shown earlier were repeated in flashbacks. The first time the scenes were shot, the director used a normal lens. When the same scenes were shown in flashback, the director used a very wide-angle lens which made the scenes much more dramatic.

Normal Lens

Every camera usually comes with a "normal" lens, which mirrors the perspective of the human eye. For instance, viewing an object using a normal lens is similar to viewing an object without a camera. Figures rendered with a normal lens will appear to be of normal size and perspective, relative to each other.

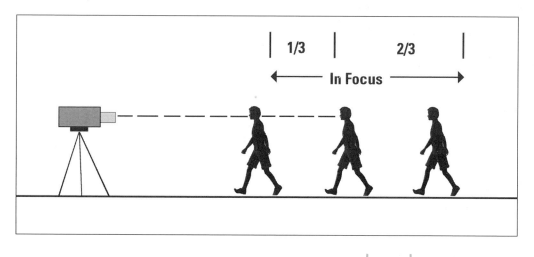

figure |6-21a|

When focusing on the middle person, the front person will be out of focus.

figure |6-21b|

Normal lens.

Wide-Angle Lens

A wide-angle lens includes a much larger area than the normal lens, exaggerating the space between near and far objects. This creates a feeling of vastness within an image. Wide-angle lenses have a short focal length, which exaggerates the distance in front of the camera. Films that have used wide-angle lenses are those that rely on panoramic shots, such as *Dances With Wolves* and *Message in a Bottle,* which opens with a panoramic shot of a boat adrift in the ocean.

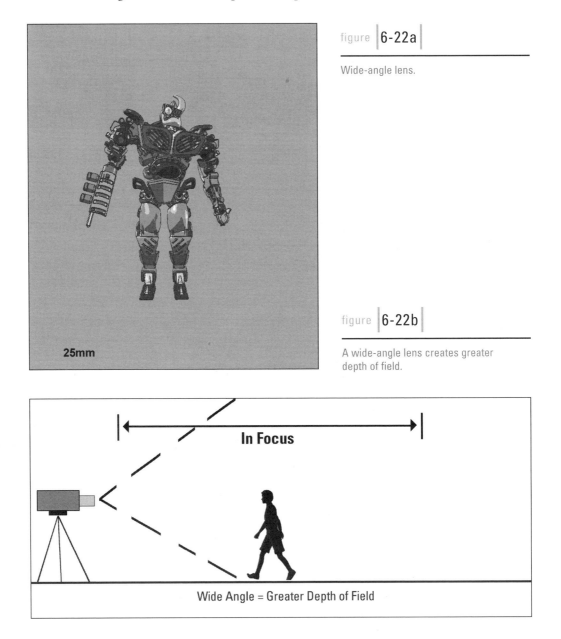

25mm

figure 6-22a

Wide-angle lens.

figure 6-22b

A wide-angle lens creates greater depth of field.

In Focus

Wide Angle = Greater Depth of Field

Wide-angle lenses are often used for establishing shots of buildings and landscapes. When using a wide-angle lens, objects in the foreground and background will both be in focus, enhancing the three-dimensional feeling of the frame. A quality of the wide-angle lens is that perspective is distorted. The wider the lens, the more distorted the image. When a subject is close to the camera, it exaggerates the size relationship. For example, a wide-angled shot of an individual kicking his foot toward the camera will create the illusion of an exaggerated foot in comparison to an undersized body.

figure |6-23|

Wide-angle lenses often distort perspective.

Courtesy of Jean-Christophe Hyacinthe

Telephoto Lens

Telephoto lenses have a shallow depth of field, compressing the foreground and background. This creates the illusion of objects appearing closer together. Any unwanted distractions in an image are thrown out of focus with a telephoto lens, making the background appear flat.

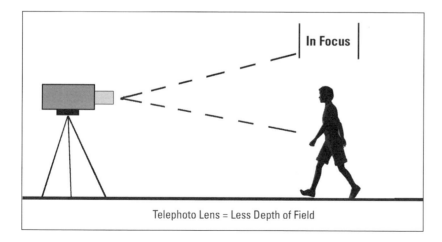

figure |6-24a|

A telephoto lens creates less depth of field.

figure | 6-24b |

Telephoto lens.

100mm

CHAPTER SUMMARY

The impression of depth within a two-dimensional storyboard design is achieved through various techniques. To understand perspective, imagine standing in front of an open window. Outside your window is the scene which you are going to draw. The horizon line runs across your view, and the parallel lines of the objects outside your window appear to meet at some point in the distance, also known as the vanishing point. Those objects that are closer to the horizon line appear more distant, whereas those objects closer to you appear larger.

Some depth cues include overlap, which is when one object is placed in front of the other, and atmospheric perspective, which is how haze or fog affects the appearance of objects. A bird's-eye view of a helicopter landing on the roof of a building is achieved by applying three-point perspective, whereas a drawing in one-point perspective allows the viewer to see an object only from straight on.

Lens choice also creates depth within an image. Shallow depth of field is when an object is in focus in the foreground, but the background is out of focus. For wide depth of field, both the foreground and background are in focus.

in review

1. What is linear perspective?

2. What happens if the picture plane moves?

3. Why is it important to make the vertical lines in the object all perpendicular to the horizon line?

4. Why draw storyboard panels in three-point perspective?

5. Define the following terms that are related to linear perspective:

   - Horizon line

   - Convergence lines

   - Vanishing point

6. What are several of the depth cues for creating storyboards in perspective?

7. How do textures add depth to a storyboard panel?

8. How does lens choice affect depth of field?

9. What is shallow depth of field?

exercises

1. Make one drawing that incorporates several different views of an office complex. Consider before you start how the views will relate to each other. The final product should be a unified whole.

2. Visit a public space such as a shopping mall. Draw the people, paying attention to their relative heights and positions in space. What other depth cues, besides size, can you note? Think overlap, texture, and foreshortening.

3. Sketch a location that mimics what you would see through the viewfinder of a wide-angle, normal, and telephoto lens.

4. Draw a building from a low-angle and high-angle point of view.

| lighting |

objectives

introduction

Lighting is a key component in the development of a visual story. It creates depth within an image, directs the focus of attention, creates mood within a scene, sets the time of day, and highlights particular objects and characters.

By working with a range of tones from pure white to black, artists can create the illusion of light in their storyboard panels. The amount of detail, however, usually depends on a production's budget, and how much time an artist has to complete a project. Regardless of budget size, every artist should have an understanding of how light affects mood and accentuates the emotions of the production's characters. This is especially important if storyboards are used to sell an idea.

LIGHTING

STORYTELLING THROUGH LIGHT

Nothing in the frame is accidental. Every element has a purpose and should be carefully considered when constructing a story. One of the most important elements is the treatment of light.

figure | 7-1 |

Stills from the 3D game *Alida*.
© Cos Russo

"*The (noir) style is rich in sensuous textures, like neon-lit streets, windshields streaked with mud, and shafts of light streaming through windows of lonely rooms. Characters are imprisoned behind ornate lattices, grillwork, drifting fog and smoke. Visual designs emphasize harsh lighting contrasts, jagged edges and violated surfaces. The tone of film noir is fatalistic and paranoid. It's suffused with pessimism, emphasizing the darker aspects of the human condition.*"

Louis Giannetti
Understanding Movies

In the early days of film, lighting was a necessity for proper exposure, but as technology advanced so did the uses for how light could enhance a story. By the 1930s and 1940s, lighting style served the purpose of making the actors and actresses appear as glamorous as possible. However, it wasn't until the emergence of the film noir genre that lighting style became a truly expressive form of visual storytelling. Many films of this style used nontraditional lighting techniques to make specific story points.

The possibilities available to enhance a visual story through a specific lighting style are limitless, from the films of the 1940s to today. Many cinematographers and lighting designers have taken the lead from film noir and have remained loyal to using light as an expressive form of defining the content and directing the viewer's gaze within a scene.

LIGHTING DESIGN FOR FILM AND 3D ANIMATION

A project's lighting design is one of the biggest artistic challenges, whether it is for film, animation, or interactive games. The general principle for lighting an animation is the same as for live action, but the process works a bit differently. Whereas lighting for live action requires the physical setup of different lighting instruments, lighting for animation is all done on the computer. Animations are manipulated with virtual lights, which is a feature of many software packages. Animation and interactive games use lighting software that requires the skill of the artist to mimic the lighting conditions of the real world. This is not an easy task since there is no standard for scripting light animation. When lights are manipulated in a 3D environment, an artist must use restraint and only move the lights when there is a clear direction on the intended mood for a scene.

Effective lighting design begins with visualization, which starts at the storyboard phase. Many storyboard artists experiment with color and light to help the director or lighting designer determine where the light and shadows should fall within a composition. By experimenting with light early in

figures **7-2a** and **7-2b**

Mood lighting.
Courtesy of David Phillips

figure **7-3**

Still from the 3D game *Alida*.
© *Cos Russo*

the process, it is likely that the director or lighting designer will be more efficient when actual production begins. A basic lighting design is the three-point lighting setup, which is the most basic lighting formula for film and animation.

Three-Point Lighting

Three-point lighting became a standard during the Classical Hollywood period of the 1930s and 1940s and continues today as the starting point for many productions. Three-point lighting is the minimum amount of lights needed to create expressive lighting. This setup includes the key light, fill light, and backlight.

figure | 7-4a |

Three-point lighting.

figure | 7-4b |

Three-point lighting.

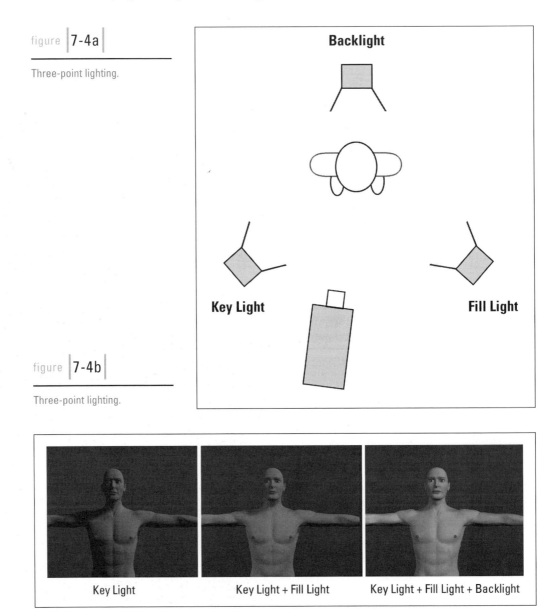

Backlight

Key Light

Fill Light

| Key Light | Key Light + Fill Light | Key Light + Fill Light + Backlight |

Key Light

The key light is the main source of light that defines the main subject or object within a shot. The key light is usually placed at a forty-five degree angle from either the right or left side of the camera. The key light illuminates the subject and creates shadows, which bring out the texture of an object or character. The sun is often considered a key light source, although direct sunlight can produce harsh shadows at certain times of the day.

Fill Light

The fill light "fills in" or softens the shadows created from the key light. The fill light is an indirect light source, which lowers the contrast between light and dark by softening the shadows.

figure | 7-5 |

Direct sunlight creates harsh shadows.

Courtesy of Jean-Christophe Hyacinthe

Backlight

Backlight is a source light that is positioned behind an object or subject. The backlight creates a highlight around the object, which allows the object to stand out from the background. Backlight gives form to such things as hair and clothing, which otherwise would fade into the background.

High- and Low-Key Lighting

The appearance of an object is usually defined by the key light, which is often considered the main light source. Outside, the sun and moon would be considered the key light. On a bright day, the sun creates harsh shadows, whereas on an overcast day, clouds diffuse the sun, which minimizes shadows and results in a softer light. Inside, key light sources include light streaming through a window, or overhead lights. Two types of key lights include high-key and low-key.

High-Key Lighting

High-key lighting is the main source of light, which conveys an overall brightness to a picture with minimal shadows. This type of lighting is used to simulate daytime. A high-key lighting design is usually seen in comedies or upbeat adventure films. High-key lighting designs are also seen in television sitcoms, news programs, and industrial videos.

High-key lighting.
Courtesy of David Phillips

Low-Key Lighting

Low-key light produces an uneven distribution of light. With a low-key lighting setup there is an abundance of shadows and concentrated areas of atmospheric light. Many areas of a low-key scene are underlit, revealing very dark areas within a frame. The most popular low-key productions are in the film noir style. Other low-key productions are serious dramas, thrillers, murder mysteries, and horror films.

Low-key lighting.
Courtesy of David Phillips

Contrast

Overall contrast is the difference between the lightest and darkest parts of a frame. By using contrast within a composition, you can focus the viewer's attention to specific areas, whereas if the entire image is sharp, the focus is on the whole.

Low Contrast

High Contrast

figures **7-8a** and **7-8b**

Low-contrast lighting.
Courtesy of Jean-Christophe Hyacinthe

High-contrast lighting.
Courtesy of the Library of Congress

High Contrast

High-contrast lighting designs emphasize the extreme differences between light and dark. This type of lighting creates dramatic and interesting images by setting off one part of an image from another. High-contrast lighting is usually seen in thrillers, horror, and suspense films. In the 1955 film *Night of the Hunter*, director Charles Laughton creates a high-contrast look through stylized visuals that play light and shadow off one another. More recent films include *Sleepy Hollow, Minority Report,* and *X2–X-Men United.* Each of these films achieves a harsh, high-contrast look.

figure **7-9**

High-contrast storyboard panel.
Courtesy of David Phillips

Low Contrast

In a low-contrast setting, there are no pure whites or blacks, but rather a range of grays. Within this type of setting, the viewer takes in the overall composition rather than its parts. Low-contrast lighting is sometimes considered boring because images are usually flat.

figure | **7-10** |

Low-contrast storyboard panel.
Courtesy of David Phillips

LIGHTING QUALITY

To understand the quality of light, and the differences between the perceived hardness and softness of light, let's go back to the example of the sun as a key light source. A sunny day creates harsh edges and shadows because it is a directional light. The opposite is true of an overcast day, which creates soft, diffused shadows because the light comes from all directions.

Hard Light

In film and animation, hard light is often used to emphasize the dramatic by illuminating a character's imperfections, which are not always flattering. Hard lighting casts clearly defined shadows and brings out the texture in objects.

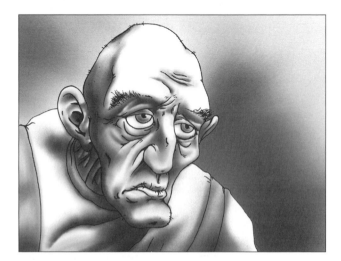

figure | **7-11a** |

Hard lighting.
Courtesy of David Phillips

figure │ 7-11b │

Hard lighting.
Courtesy of Jean-Christophe Hyacinthe

Soft Light

Soft light softens an object. For example, many actresses of the 1940s were shot in soft, diffused light, which evens out skin tone and hides any imperfections, such as wrinkles and blemishes.

figures │ 7-12a and 7-12b │

Soft lighting.
(Left) Courtesy of David Phillips
(Right) Courtesy of Jean-Christophe Hyacinthe

RENDERING LIGHT WITHIN THE STORYBOARD FRAME

When drawing storyboard frames, the kind of shadows that you create are going to depend on the quality of light. If a scene calls for hard light, shadows will be harsh. Drawing hard edges requires the use of a sharp drawing tool. Suppose you are going to draw a person with one light source falling harshly on one side of the face. Look at where the highlights and shadows fall. Start picking out the prominent shadows and notice how they form patterns. Applying dark shadows to these areas brings out depth within your image. Highlights are the opposite of shadows. They reflect the actual light source. When drawing highlights, you need to be aware of the object's surface. For example, if the surface is smooth, like the hood of a car, highlights will be bright, but if the surface is rough, the highlights will be more diffuse.

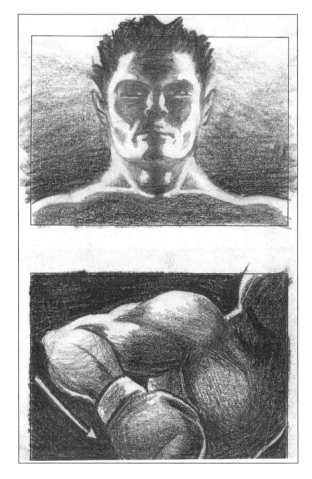

DIRECTION OF LIGHT

A light source may come from many different directions, including the side, front, back, below, and above. The direction of a light source changes the pattern of light and shadow, which affects the mood of a scene. The direction of light is important because it casts shadows that can emphasize such things as texture and details.

Frontal Lighting

Frontal lighting creates a flat image with barely any distinction between the foreground and background elements. With frontal lighting, there are minimal shadows and texture, which tends to create a boring composition. Frontal lighting is good for showing the color relationships in a scene. For example, rendering the historic building with a bed of tulips in the foreground would work well with a frontal lighting setup.

figure |7-14|

Frontal lighting.
Courtesy of David Phillips

| TIP |

To understand lighting, you need to do your homework. Look through photography books, and observe the lighting in restaurants and stores, as well as light in the morning compared to the afternoon and evenings. Observing light in various situations will help you to grasp how light looks at different times of the day, and how certain lighting designs affect mood.

Side Lighting

A strong contrast is created when one side of an object is brightly lit and the other side is in shadows. Side lighting creates a three-dimensional effect because of the shadows made on one side of an object. Side lighting is often used to convey a protagonist's struggle by being half in the light, half in the shadows. For example, in the film *Fight Club*, the main protagonist, Jack, is filmed with his face partially obscured by dark shadows, conveying to the audience his conflict between right and wrong. Side lighting also brings out the detail and texture of objects, such as the leaves on a tree, or the creases in a wrinkled face.

figure |7-15|

Side lighting.
Courtesy of David Phillips

Backlighting

Backlighting is when the source of light is behind an object or character that comes forward. Backlighting often creates the illusion of depth by separating the background from the subject.

figure | 7-16 |

Backlighting.
Courtesy of David Phillips

"To me, making a film is like resolving conflicts between light and dark, cold and warmth, blue and orange, or other contrasting colors. There should be a sense of energy, or change of movement. A sense that time is going on—light becomes night, which reverts to morning. Life becomes death. Making a film is like documenting a journey and using light in the style that best suits that particular picture . . . the concept behind it."

Vittorio Storaro,
Cinematographer
The Last Emperor

One of the most dramatic forms of backlighting is the silhouette. This effect shows no color or texture; only the shape of the subject is visible. When using silhouettes, the audience is usually kept from seeing the entire scene; this creates a mysterious quality, which conveys mood.

Underlighting

Underlighting comes from below an individual or object and produces odd-looking shadows. This type of lighting illuminates the bottom half of a figure and shades the top, making a character appear malevolent and sinister. Underlighting is often seen in horror films and thrillers.

figure | 7-17 |

Underlighting.
Courtesy of David Phillips

REALISTIC AND DRAMATIC LIGHTING

How much realism should be considered when envisioning a lighting design?

Most productions strive to create scenes that look realistic. Such pragmatic designs suggest to the audience that the lighting design occurs naturally, and it often appears invisible to the audience. Light from candles, lamps, and fireplaces is frequently used to enhance a realistic setting. Video games, films, and television use realistic lighting designs to make characters appear more natural. In the film *Like Water for Chocolate,* many scenes are lit by candles and light streaming through windows to give the film a soft appearance. Because of this realistic approach to lighting, the characters often have a warm golden appearance, making them look beautiful even when the cruelest acts are occurring.

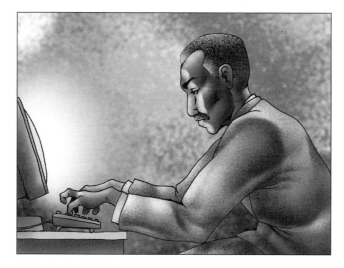

figure 7-18

Realistic lighting.
Courtesy of David Phillips

In contrast to naturalistic lighting, a stylistic approach makes imagery appear more dramatic. Stylized lighting is often used to accentuate mood.

The roots of dramatic lighting in early cinema can be found in German Expressionism. Films such as *The Cabinet of Doctor Caligari*, *Metropolis*, and *Dracula* concentrated on the heavy use of light and dark contrast to suggest the inner state of its characters, the supernatural, and the craziness of the world.

Stylized lighting is popular with many of today's film directors and is now becoming more so among game designers. Although many game designers use static lighting, games such as *Lara Croft Tomb Raider III*, an action adventure game from Eidos, features dramatic lighting effects to enhance the overall quality of the game. Many game designers use dramatic lighting to direct a player's attention to specific attributes of the game, which can be used to influence character choices.

figure 7-19

Stylized lighting.
Courtesy of David Phillips

COLOR

The color palette plays an important role in the visual style of a film, animation, and game design. Color often creates a sense of time and space, establishes mood and atmosphere, and provides emotional impact. Bright colors, for instance, add energy and have a dramatic impact, while lighter hues impart a harmonious and stable look.

figure 7-20

Meaning of color diagram.

THE MEANING OF COLOR	
Black	Authority, power, evil, pessimism
Red	Optimism, sex, danger, aggression, energy, excitement, passion, fire, love, dynamism
Green	Envy, fertility, growth, money, good luck, healing, success
Pink	Tranquility, love, flirtatiousness, softness, delicacy, sweetness
Yellow	Cheerfulness, joy, optimism, happiness, energy
Orange	Joy, creativity, energy, encouragement, success
Purple	Royalty, power, nobility, luxury, spirituality, wisdom, mystery, wealth
Blue	Calmness, truth, peace, harmony, confidence, wisdom, loyalty, healing, water, stability
White	Innocence, purity, sterility
Gray	Neutrality, corporate, quality, practicality
Brown	Stability, endurance, simplicity, friendship

The cinematographer and production designer usually choose the color palette, based on what the director wants. Many directors use color as a visual or symbolic motif in their films. For example, in the 2002 film *Frida*, when Kahlo wanted to hide something, director Julie Taymor used bold colors to represent a particular time period while contrasting the frame with dark shadows.

In Spike Lee's *Do the Right Thing*, the color palette combines brilliant colors of red, orange, and yellow to signify the sweltering heat and racial tensions between African and Italian Americans. In the film *Far from Heaven*, director Todd Haynes establishes an upbeat mood in the first half of the movie by bathing the main protagonist Cathy, a 1950s housewife, in crisp, rich colors. As Cathy's world falls apart midway through the film, it's as if the color is drained from her and her surroundings.

Many filmmakers, game designers, and animators use color as a visual or symbolic motif in their projects. In *The Thin Red Line,* the green foliage, which represents life, is used in stark contrast with red, which symbolizes death.

The Basics of Color

To create meaning in a production, however, you must first understand the basics of color. This begins by understanding the principles of the color wheel, which is made up of twelve colors.

All colors are made up of three primary colors: red, yellow, and blue. The secondary colors—orange, violet, and green—lie between the primary colors and are considered a result of combining two primary colors. For instance, yellow combined with red equals orange, and yellow mixed with blue makes green. Lastly, there are six intermediate colors, also called tertiary colors, which are a mixture of one primary color and one secondary color.

"Throughout the film, we tried to fill the top of the frame with heavy objects to create a sense of compression and claustrophobia. When Sullivan and his son are released into the second and third acts of the movie, there's a sense that they're cut adrift in a mythic, empty landscape."

Sam Mendes, Director
Road to Perdition

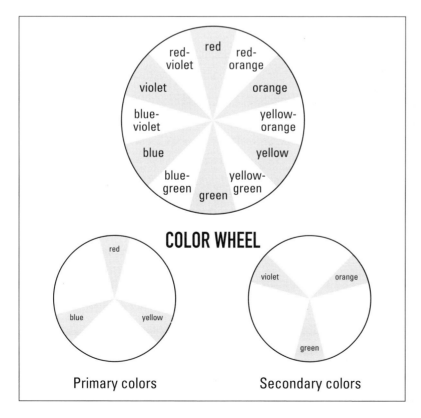

figure 7-21

Color wheel.

Colors that contrast are opposite each other on the color wheel and go together quite well, such as red and green, purple and yellow, blue and orange. These colors complement each other because they have the greatest contrast, which makes for a bold and dramatic look.

We can also think of colors as warm or cold. Warm colors include red, orange, and yellow. These colors are considered warm because they remind us of hot things, such as fire or the sun. Warm colors often produce feelings of excitement, intimacy, and happiness. Cool colors include blue, green, and purple and often suggest a coldness or starkness. The general perception is that warmer colors advance within a composition while cooler colors recede into the background. There are the rare exceptions when a cooler color such as blue will stand out against a warm background. This, however, takes quite a bit of manipulation on the part of the art director or cinematographer.

CHAPTER SUMMARY

Lighting is an integral technique to any production; it helps shape the tone of a film, creates depth by separating foreground and background elements, and sets the time of day. To understand the quality of light, you should understand why the sun is considered a key light source. If the sun is bright in the sky, it creates harsh shadows, but if the day is overcast, the clouds diffuse the sun, which minimizes shadows and results in a very soft light. Many productions use hard and soft light to emphasize the mood of a scene; harsh light often conveys a dark and ominous environment, and soft light hides any imperfections.

The direction of light determines where light and shadows fall on an object. A side light creates shadows on one side of an object, which creates a three-dimensional effect. A frontal light, on the other hand, minimizes shadows and creates a flat image. The most dramatic direction of light is backlighting. A dramatic form of backlighting creates a silhouette of an object or character, and often separates foreground and background elements.

The color palette plays an important role in many productions. It often sets the tone for a narrative. Cool color palettes, for instance, are often used to set an austere tone, whereas warmer palettes often signify excitement or even anger.

TIP

If you render a composition that takes place at sunrise, the colors of the morning are warm and tend toward the red and orange side. Shadows at this time of day may look slightly blue in hue. As the sun climbs during the day, there is a greater amount of contrast between the blue sky and sun. Contrast between colors will be at its peak at high noon, and as the sun goes down, shadows become more prominent, bringing out textures.

in review

1. What is the difference between high-key and low-key lighting?

2. When should you use hard lighting?

3. How does lighting shape the mood of a scene?

4. How does the direction of light affect a scene?

5. What time of day creates harsh shadows on an object?

6. What type of light creates a flat image with minimal shadows?

7. What type of light creates silhouettes?

8. What is the difference between warm and cool color palettes?

exercises

1. Pick a scene from a movie and study it. What direction is the light source coming from? Where do the highlights and shadows fall? What is the color scheme? Does the scene use high-contrast or low-contrast lighting? How does the lighting design affect mood? Write a short analysis of your findings.

2. Re-create the direction of light using an egg and a simple table lamp. Position the light to the side, front, above, back, and underneath the egg. Draw where the shadows and highlights fall on the egg.

3. Study several scenes from films or animation—with the sound turned off—and pay attention to whether they have warm and/or cool color palettes. What type of mood do you think the director is trying to convey? What emotion do you think the director wants you to feel? What does the color tell you about the scene?

continuity

Courtesy of J. Allen McFadden

objectives

Explain the basic rules of continuity

Explain how continuity establishes order

Understand how shots are combined to create meaning

Explore noncontinuous shots such as the montage and jump cut

introduction

One of my favorite opening scenes is from the film *Memento*. It begins with an extreme close shot of a photograph being rapidly flapped back and forth as a picture of a murdered man slowly fades to nothingness. I was intrigued. Who is the man waving the picture, and more importantly who is the dead guy? Ultimately the picture fades to white and the main protagonist is revealed holding the photograph.

Editing is a central aspect of *Memento*. The film is shot in reverse order and relies on editing techniques such as superimposing images onto the next and flash forward images, which tell the story from the last frame of the film to the very first frame. As a storyboard artist, it is important to understand the editing process, and, most importantly, continuity editing, which is an editing style used to create programs that flow continuously from beginning to end. This may seem misleading since continuity is about splicing together shots of various frame sizes and camera angles. There may be as many as a dozen cuts within a one-minute period; however, these edits are "invisible" if the editor does his job well. If continuity is achieved, audiences will not notice the edits but rather will see the story as a continuous whole. If the editor has not achieved continuity, however, the spectator's illusion of seeing consecutive action will be interrupted.

A good director or designer will consider continuity at the storyboard phase. Each frame that is sketched is evaluated and judged, as the story is composed shot by shot. Essential details are considered, including the pacing and transitions, to establish the visual flow of the project.

This chapter looks specifically at techniques used to achieve continuity, whether for film, animation, or cinematic sequences in games.

CONTINUITY

BASIC PRINCIPLE OF CONTINUITY

The basic principle of continuity is to tell a story that develops through the interactions of its characters. If you look at most films, you will notice that many are based on continuity editing, which allows the director to create seamless sequences that flow from one shot to the next. Let's say, for instance, you are watching a baseball movie such as *Bull Durham*. A real-life baseball game is nine innings long, lasting several hours. Film reality, however, shows a game that takes place in only a few minutes. As you develop each scene, you may compress, or in some instances, stretch time. If a sequence is too fast, the audience will not understand what is happening; if the story is too slow, audiences become bored. Let's look at an example.

- Man looks at watch, agitated (2 seconds)
- Woman walks down the stairs and greets husband with a wooden kiss (5 seconds)
- The couple rushes out of the house (3 seconds)
- The couple pulls out of the driveway (3 seconds)
- The couple drives down various streets (8 seconds)
- Couple waits at a light (3 seconds)
- Car pulls up to a theater (3 seconds)
- Couple waits in a long line (5 seconds)
- Couple reaches ticket booth as sold out sign is put in the window (5 seconds)
- Man throws his hands into the air and walks away (3 seconds)

If the above sequence was played out on the screen in real time, the audience would surely lose interest. There are too many nonessential details, such as the drive down various streets, waiting at the light, etc. What are the most important shots leading up to the sold out show? The role of continuity in the above scenario is to compress the amount of time it really takes to get from the house to the theater to accomplish the task of buying tickets. You want to cut out anything that is not pertinent to understanding the story line to keep it moving. Audiences have the imagination to fill in the missing pieces. By compressing time, the above sequence may look something like this:

- Man looks at watch, annoyed (2 seconds)
- Couple rushes out the door (3 seconds)
- Couple in car (3 seconds)
- Couple pulls up to theater (3 seconds)
- Couple steps up to the ticket booth as a sold out sign flashes in the window (5 seconds)
- Man throws his hands into the air and walks away (3 seconds)

figure |8-1|

Continuity editing and compressing time.

Courtesy of J. Allen McFadden

Creating the illusion of continuous action in "reel time" can be tricky, especially when dealing with hundreds, if not thousands, of shots that vary in frame size and camera position. If a production achieves continuity, the audience will not *see* the manipulation of time and space. They will be swept up in the narrative even if the story jumps suddenly to the future or back in time. One of the most outrageous leaps in time is in the Stanley Kubrick film *2001: A Space Odyssey*. The film begins with a prehistoric ape throwing a bone into the air and on its descent, it transitions to a space shuttle about to dock at a space station. Quite a bold leap in time, but it works.

Several techniques that can be applied to create continuity include proper transitions, matching eye lines and action, and applying the 180-degree rule to your work.

figure |8-2|

Storyboard panels from the independent film *AKA*.

Courtesy of Invision Films

The Line of Action

The line of action, also known as the 180-degree rule, is one of the most important continuity tools because it helps to organize camera angles and movement in a consistent screen direction. The line of action is an imaginary line that runs right in front of the camera or the direction the eyes are looking (line of sight), which gives the audience a sense of direction for the scene.

The easiest way to see how the line of action works is to render a profile shot of two people standing across from each other. The line of action is drawn between the two individuals. Once the line is in place, there is a space of 180-degrees (or a half circle) where shots can be rendered. As an artist, you want to make sure that you capture the action of a shot from the same side of the line to maintain consistency. If the line is crossed, one character might end up looking at the backside of another character's head. What if you want to show separate locations of two people talking on the phone with each other? In such situations, you still want to establish an imaginary line between the characters. Therefore, when cutting from one character to the next, the characters should be facing each other, even if they are in separate locations.

figure 8-3

The line of action. Establish the line of action by drawing a line between two people having a conversation.

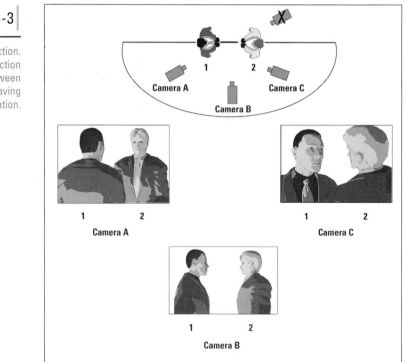

Crossing the Line

Once the line of action is established, there are several occasions when a character or object may cross the line. One approach is to keep the camera moving. A dolly or crane shot can move over the established line, as long as the movement is continuous. You may also cross the line if an object or person moves across the line. Let's say two people are having coffee when one of the characters gets up and moves to a new position. Once the character establishes eye contact with the seated character, you have established a new line.

The camera may cross the line of action when a new sight line for a character is established. Let's say two characters are lounging around, watching a football game. If the camera cuts away to a third person entering the room and one of the characters seated turns to acknowledge the third person (establishing a new sight line), you may cross the line and establish a new one.

figure | 8-4 |

Maintaining consistent screen direction.

What if you have a scene where the main character is rushing through a crowded subway station looking for a kidnapped girl? In such a situation, you may want to cross the line to establish a frenetic or disorienting pace. By crossing the line, you will end up with several shots that showcase the main character running back and forth through the subway station, even though in reality the character is moving in the same direction. Be aware, however; there is a very fine line between conveying a character's confusion and confusing your audience.

Screen Direction

When rendering storyboards, it is important to plan the direction a person or object moves or looks toward. If a character is facing in one direction in the first shot, and the opposite direction in the second shot, continuity will be jeopardized. This often confuses viewers as to the intent of the scene, especially when there are dozens of shots that make up a scene. A good director will rely on the shot list and storyboards to maintain a consistent screen direction.

Several different types of screen direction include neutral, constant, and contrasting direction.

Neutral Screen Direction

Neutral screen direction is movement toward or away from the camera; it shows only the front or backside of a person or object. One of the most common shots we see of neutral screen direction is when a character walks directly toward the camera and blacks out the lens. Neutral screen direction provides impact and is quite dynamic because the character or object appears to increase in size as it moves closer to the camera. For instance, a shot of the bad guy running straight at the camera will often jolt an audience.

figure | 8-5 |

Neutral screen direction is movement toward or away from the camera.

Constant Screen Direction

Constant screen direction shows movement in one direction only. Let's say a downtown bus is traveling its daily route through the city. You would storyboard the progression of shots of the bus going in the same direction. If you cut to a shot of the same bus traveling in the opposite direction, this will confuse the audience because the bus appears to be moving back to its starting point.

The same can be said of subjects entering and exiting a frame. Subjects should move in the same direction whether they are moving left-to-right or right-to-left. One technique to maintain a consistent screen direction is to establish a line of action and then position the camera to one side of the line. Once the line and the camera are established, screen direction will be maintained.

figure | 8-6 |

The bus moves in a constant screen direction.

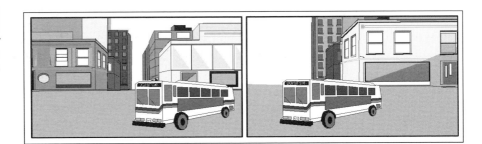

Contrasting Screen Direction

Contrasting screen direction is when a person comes into the frame from one direction and leaves in the opposite direction. This is often called left-to-right and right-to-left movement. In figure 8-7, a businessman leaves his office and walks left-to-right toward his home. Therefore, movement from home to the office would be a right-to-left movement.

Left to right movement from work to home.   Right to left movement from home to work.

figure **8-7**

Continuity of direction.

Opposing screen direction is also established by showing two objects, or people, moving toward each other. Suppose two tanks are headed for each other on a collision course. To create tension, the timing of the shots gets faster, and the shot framing tighter, as the tanks accelerate toward each other until contact.

figure **8-8**

Contrasting screen direction shows vehicles moving in opposing directions toward each other.

Shot/Reverse Shot

The shot/reverse shot is a common technique used to create continuity between two or more characters. It allows the audience to follow the action between characters as camera angles and framing changes. The simplest form of the shot/reverse shot is staging a conversation between two characters. Let's say Mr. Smith and Ms. Vargas are in the kitchen discussing dinner plans, as in figure 8-9. How does this scene work as a shot/reverse shot?

figure | 8-9 |

One of the most popular shot/reverse shots is an over-the-shoulder shot of two people talking.

You may want to set up an initial shot that establishes the location and the characters. Once established, draw the line of action between Mr. Smith and Ms. Vargas. The imaginary line allows the camera to be positioned anywhere on one side of the line, to capture the conversation between the two characters. A typical shot/reverse shot frames characters over the shoulder. Thus, if the camera is behind Mr. Smith, who is looking right at Ms. Vargas, the camera is behind Mr. Smith's left shoulder. In the reverse shot, the camera is behind Ms. Vargas's right shoulder, as she looks left.

Match on Action

Match on action is the illusion that the action continues uninterrupted, even though the camera positions may have changed from one shot to the next. To create a match cut, everything at the end of the first shot must closely match with the action at the beginning of the next shot. It is generally easier to create a match cut by noticeably changing the size of the frame and cutting on the movement. For instance cutting on the movement of the character taking off his glasses, as in figure 8-10, appears fluid as the director cuts from a full shot to a medium shot.

When matching action, you should only cut after the audience understands the visual information that is being delivered. If a shot is too fast, the audience will not have time to absorb the details, and if the shot is too long, the audience will be irked.

figure |8-10|

Match on action from a full shot to a medium shot of character taking off sunglasses.
Courtesy of Invision Films

Eye Line Match

The eye line match creates order and meaning within the story space by matching eye lines between characters or what a character is looking at.

Put simply, if a person looks off-screen in the first frame, the audience will expect to be shown what the character sees in the next shot. If a character looks screen left at a character off-screen, then an imaginary line of sight will be drawn between him and the off-screen character. By obeying the line of sight, the characters will look toward each other, maintaining eye lines.

figure |8-11|

Eye line match.
Courtesy of Invision Films

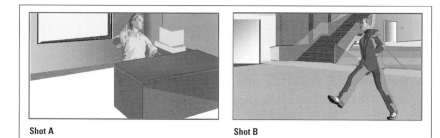

Shot A Shot B

figure |8-12|

Shot A shows a man looking off-screen. Shot B shows the audience what the character is looking at, which in this case is another character.

Cutaways

The cutaway technique is used to manipulate time and space. The cutaway should be related to the main action, but not a part of it. For example, while two boxers exchange blows in the ring, you might cut away to jeering fans, or perhaps a refreshments vendor.

figure |8-13|

A cutaway cuts from the main action to a secondary action.

Cutaways allow the director to make minor shifts in time. If a character is robbing a convenience store clerk, for instance, a cutaway to the reactions of store patrons will allow the robber to have the money and be ready to make his getaway. By cutting away from the main action, we do not need to see every action of the clerk opening the register and putting the money into a bag.

Cutaways also reveal information about the personality of its characters. A cutaway shot to a cluttered bookshelf of self-help books could reveal personality traits, as do a favorite stuffed animal, or a medicine cabinet full of vitamins.

Cut-Ins

figure |8-14|

A cut-in focuses on the primary action by cutting into the main action.

Cut-ins focus on the primary action of a scene. Rather than cutting away from the main action, the cut-in shot narrows our view to a smaller portion of the main action, providing dramatic emphasis.

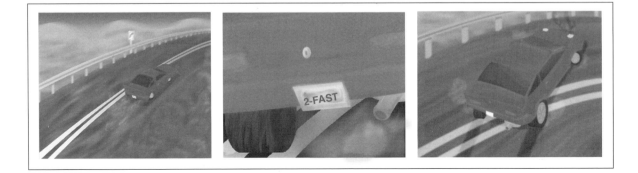

If the main action is a baseball game, a cut-in could be a bat connecting to a baseball. The dramatic action of the bat hitting the ball in the smaller action must match what is being shown in the larger scene. If it does not match, you will have a jump cut in which the figure appears to move but the background does not.

Crosscutting

Crosscutting, also called parallel editing, manipulates both time and space. Action that is happening at the same time is intercut so the audience may see the parallel action.

Crosscutting is often used to intensify the drama and to provide suspense in a film or animation. How many times have you witnessed scenes of the bad guy about to kill his next victim as the hero races to the hideout? These two independent scenes are edited together to keep the audience on the edge of their seats as they wonder if the hero will make it in time.

An excellent use of crosscutting is shown in the film *The Godfather*. The sequence between the baptism of Michael Corleone's nephew crosscuts with the Corleone mobsters preparing for and ultimately committing murder. Although the sequence lasts for six minutes, it is fairly fast paced.

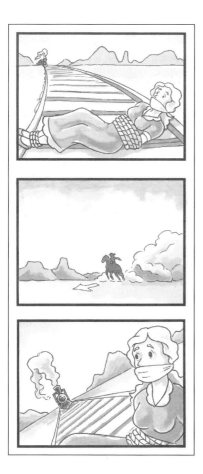

figure | 8-15 |

Crosscutting manipulates both time and space by editing together independent scenes.

Transitions

A transition is a narrative device that links together two different shots that may change in time, place, location, or characters. Transitions contribute to the pacing of a production, whether it is lyrical or abrupt. There are several different types of transitions, including the dissolve, cut, and fade.

Dissolves

The dissolve is when pieces of filmstrip are superimposed onto each other. Dissolves can be any length and are often used to show either a time lapse or a location change. For example, shot #1 in figure 8-17 is a person exiting a limousine. The shot slowly dissolves to shot #2 of the character on the train platform. We can assume from the dissolve that the man waiting on the train platform is the same man that was getting out of the limousine.

figure

Dissolves are represented in storyboards as two panels that are joined together with two diagonal lines in the form of an X.

figure 8-17

Dissolve transition.

Cuts

The cut is an unobtrusive and frequently used transition in terms of storytelling. Over 90 percent of films use cuts as a transition to connect shots together. Most audiences do not even notice when a program cuts to different angles or framing within a scene. A logical cut may include a wide shot of a building that cuts to a full shot of the building door. The cut is effective for compressing time. A four-hour wedding, for example, can be compressed to a few minutes by using cuts.

Fades

Fades are used to denote a passage of time and should not be used in the present tense. Fades are usually very subtle as the screen fades in or out from black. (If it fades to white, it is often called a white-out).

A fade-in is used to ease the audience into a setting by starting in black, and gradually lightening up the setting to full brightness. A fade-out is usually the last shot of a scene that gradually disappears into darkness. Fades are often used to separate scenes or to change locations.

Wipes

Wipes function the same way as the cut, transitioning from one shot to the next, but here it pushes one image off the screen with another image. This showy technique was quite popular during the 1930s and 1940s, but went out of fashion shortly after World War II. The wipe made a resurgence in the 1970s with the release of *Star Wars*, and can be seen in a handful of films today.

Jump Cuts

Jump cuts are the opposite of continuity shots, using abrupt changes in movement to disrupt the illusion of a continuous flow of action. A jump cut can be achieved between shots by maintaining the background and abruptly changing a character's position. In the film *Dark Blue*, the character played by Kurt Russell appears to jump from a bed to the window, to a chair, etc., to communicate the passage of time. In such situations, the story has "jumped" over some of the action.

Jump cuts are also achieved when character framing is the same from one shot to the next, but the camera has moved its position.

figure | 8-18 |

Jump cuts.

Montage

Cinematic montage is a series of images that are juxtaposed to create meaning by evoking an emotional response. The shots contain information relating to a single idea or theme. Music videos are often assembled around montage sequences of a band or singer. In such scenarios, the rhythm and pacing of the video often depends on the structure of the song.

Let's say you have two separate shots. The first shot, shot A, is of a group of students languishing over an exam in a classroom. Shot B is of someone sleeping in bed. The shots are unrelated in both time and space, yet when they are juxtaposed with one another, they create meaning. The two shots lead the audience to believe that the character in bed has overslept on exam day.

The montage style was developed in the 1920s by Soviet filmmakers such as Sergi Eisenstein and Dziga Vertov. One of the most famous montage sequences is of the Odessa Steps from Eisenstein's *Battleship Potemkin*. The images include boots of the soldiers stomping down steps, a mother screaming, a baby carriage rolling out of control, a broken umbrella, a woman's bleeding eye, and close-ups of frightened faces. These edits include shots that vary in length to build the rhythm of the sequence, which ultimately climaxes with the massacre and failure of the Russian revolution.

figure | 8-19 |

Elements of a montage sequence.

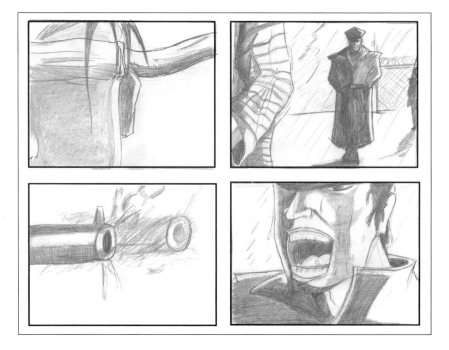

CHAPTER SUMMARY

Continuity editing works to join shots together to create dramatic meaning. If an editor has done her job well, the audience will not notice how shots of various frame sizes and angles are spliced together to tell the story. Instead the audience will see the story as a continuous whole of uninterrupted action. There are several techniques to create continuity, including the shot/reverse shot, the 180-degree rule, match on action, and the eye line match. The 180-degree rule organizes camera angles and movement in a consistent screen direction by capturing the action of a shot from the same side.

When rendering storyboards, it is important to plan the direction a person or object will move or look. If a character is facing in one direction in the first shot, and the opposite direction in the second shot, continuity will be forfeited. This often confuses viewers as to the intent of the scene. Constant screen direction shows movement from one direction only, whereas contrasting screen direction shows opposing movement.

Screen direction is the direction in which a character or object looks or moves. This is probably one of the easiest things to learn, yet one of the simplest mistakes to make in storyboarding. In consecutive shots, a person should be looking or walking in a certain direction; continuity is shattered if that person looks or walks in the opposing direction. The line of action dictates screen direction, which is an imaginary line that extends from the camera to a subject. If storyboard artists cross the imaginary line of action, audiences become confused.

Continuity editing is also achieved through the shot/reverse shot, which follows the action between characters as the camera angles and framing changes. One of the most common techniques is the eye line match, which creates order by matching eye lines between characters or what they are looking at.

Creating the story space is also achieved through the use of transitions. There are several different types of transitions, including the cut, wipe, and dissolve. Cuts are the most basic and frequently used of the transitions, whereas wipes are quite showy as one image is pushed off by another. The dissolve links two shots together to show a passage of time.

Two editing techniques that oppose continuity are the montage and the jump cut. Montage is the process of combining unrelated shots to create meaning. In jump cuts, a character is framed the same from one shot to the next, but the camera has moved. Jump cuts are the opposite of continuity editing because abrupt changes in movement disregard the 180-degree rule.

in review

1. What is the 180-degree rule?

2. When can you cross the line of action without breaking continuity?

3. What happens if continuity is sacrificed?

4. What is the difference between the cut-in and the cutaway?

5. What is continuity editing?

6. How do jump cuts differ from continuity editing?

7. What are several different types of transitions?

8. What is the difference between an eye line match and a shot/reverse shot?

exercises

1. Pick a short scene (two minutes) from *Casablanca*. Count the number of edits. Replay the scene, stopping at each edit point. Write down a description of the shot and the shot immediately following it. What did each edit communicate?

2. Many music videos are based on the montage approach of combining shots to create meaning. In this exercise, you will create your own music video in twenty-four shots using a digital camera. When it is complete, provide an analysis for why you chose each shot and how each shot you selected created meaning.

notes

animation, film, and special effects

objectives

Understand the difference between live action and animation storyboards

Explore the relationship between the storytelling process and story art

Learn the process for creating storyboards for television animation

introduction

Since the early days of Disney, storyboards have become an indispensable tool to the production process, guiding projects for both animated shorts and feature films.

Similar to film storyboards, the animated storyboard shows how a story visually unfolds by staging camera placement and virtual lights, in addition to defining the look of the characters and the environments. But whereas storyboards for film are rendered mainly for special effects and action sequences, storyboards for animation are followed much more closely, and sketched for every shot. For example, if a character runs into a building, you need to show more than the starting and ending points of the action. Several in between frames are necessary to convey the personality and emotion of the character, including how the character walks, its facial expressions, and reactions. But this is not the first step for story artists. They work alongside the writers of a screenplay to flesh out story ideas. It is at this stage that story issues are dealt with, before fine-tuning the staging of a sequence. This is somewhat different from production storyboards for film, which are usually rendered once the screenplay is finalized.

This chapter looks specifically at the relationship between storyboards, the storytelling process, and the nuances that make up the film and animation production storyboard.

STORYBOARDS AND FEATURE ANIMATION

The relationship between the storytelling and art departments has been in existence since Disney Studios organized its first story department in the early 1930s. When storyboards were first introduced, "story men" or "gagmen" would write the script underneath each storyboard panel as the story line was developed. Not much has changed since the Golden Era of animation. Today, story artists often work in tandem with writers to flesh out the emotional goals of the story and the personalities of its characters. The storyboard allows the creative team to take a step back and see how well the story flows from one scene to the next. If parts of the story are confusing, or if the emphasis is not in the right place, the story artists will need to go back and revise their work.

? DID YOU KNOW

It took over two years to create the storyboards for Dreamwork's *The Prince of Egypt.*

Once story sketches for a scene are complete, they are pinned to a corkboard for the story meeting. Either the story artist or the director will "act out" the scene's storyboards, which are both analyzed and criticized by the team. Therefore, it is important that animation storyboards show a character's actions and personal eccentricities, such as twisting a strand of hair or furrowing a brow.

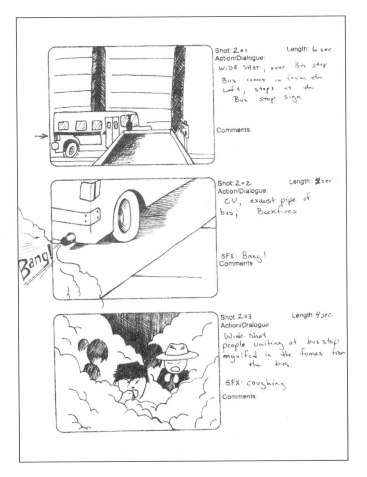

figure | 9-1a |

Staging the action at the storyboard phase allows directors to experiment with composition.

Courtesy of Richard Nevendorf III

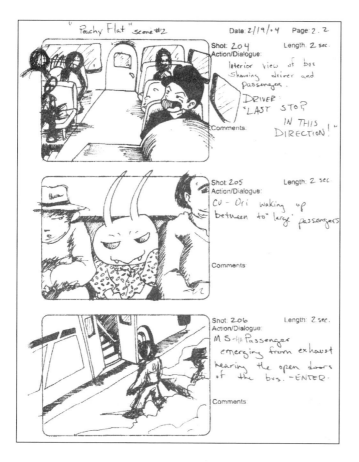

figure | 9-1b |

Staging the action at the storyboard phase allows directors to experiment with composition.
Courtesy of Richard Nevendorf III

It is here that changes are made to the story structure, which includes adding and deleting gags and jokes, and refining the plot of the story. This process may be repeated a number of times before the director is satisfied with the visual outcome of the story. Once there is final approval for a storyboard sequence, the storyboard artist tightens the layout. This includes blocking the action, camera framing, and creating the illusion of movement. Determining the staging early in the preproduction process allows animators to experiment with the composition, which would be too expensive during production.

Preparing Storyboard Panels

A feature screenplay has as many as forty to sixty scenes; this translates into several thousand storyboard sketches. Artists are assigned to storyboard specific scenes because of the multitude of sketches that need to be rendered for an entire feature animation. Several artists may work on the same sequence; therefore, it becomes imperative for each artist to follow the guidelines provided by the director.

| TIP |

A person should be able to understand visually what is happening in a storyboard sequence without reading the panel descriptions. If not, you may need to go back to your panels and make adjustments.

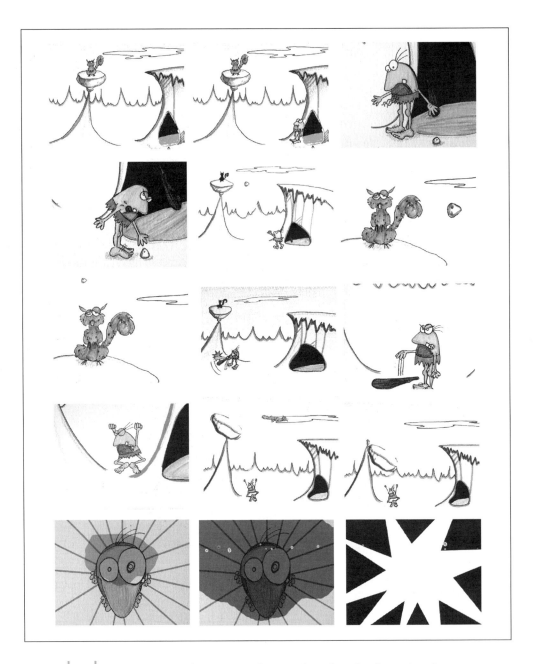

Similar to live action, the storyboard artist for animation captures a character's performance through timing, movement, and shot composition. By experimenting with these areas in your storyboard panels, you should come up with several interesting ways to execute your ideas. For instance, in figure 9-3 the main protagonist (a purple monkey) is being chased through the forest by a wolf. To capture the action of the characters, thumbnails and roughs were created that experimented with different shot compositions for how to best express the action and mood of the scene.

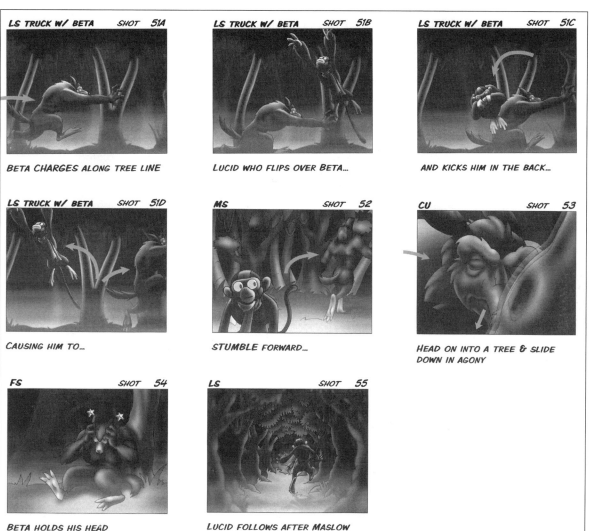

figure 9-3

Previsualizing an animation sequence.
Courtesy of David Phillips

Scene Checklist

Several questions to consider as you plan an animation scene include:

- What is the purpose of the scene?
- What idea am I trying to communicate to my audience?
- What type of shots do I need to impart the urgency of the scene?
- Is the emphasis in the right place within a shot?
- Are there a variety of close-shots? Long shots?

Besides experimenting with shot composition, you must also work on pacing your shots. Pacing is probably one of the most difficult aspects of animation, especially when it comes to a character's performance. If the

Long shot of Rusty as he dives into mud

Rusty POV

FS as Rusty jumps up from the mud

Start MCS of Rusty Dolly in

Dolly end of an ECU of Rusty

figure 9-4

Vary shots to stimulate audience interest.

Courtesy of Dorian Soto

pacing is too slow, the audience becomes bored, but if it is too fast, oftentimes the audience becomes confused. Think about the personality of your characters. How would they react in certain situations? Quick movements often grab our interest, but it is the slow movements that help build the story. Let's say you have a confrontation between two characters. You may want to keep the pacing fast to surprise the audience. To do this, you may choose quick cuts of shots of various frame sizes, as in figure 9-4.

When formatting the storyboard panels, make sure to include both scene and shot numbers, in addition to panel descriptions of the action and dialogue. A typical animation script may warrant several thousand panels to tell a story. Therefore, to save time and resources, backgrounds are only drawn when there is a location change.

STORY REEL

Once storyboards are approved, they are assembled into a story reel (which will be discussed further in Chapter 13). Story reels are moving storyboards that reflect the pacing of the animation and what it will look like.

When creating a story reel, the camera department shoots each frame and inputs it into a software program such as After Effects. Here the artist manipulates the camera framing and simple movement such as pans and zooms. A rough voice track is then recorded, which the animator synchs to the storyboard panels for timing purposes. As artwork for a sequence is finished, the animator will replace the story reel images with the different stages of final artwork, including rough, refined, and final animation.

Creating the story reel allows the creative team to experiment with pacing of individual shots to see how the story flows before resources are committed to animating. According to Mark Vaz, "The story reel is like the foundation and substructure of the house; without that foundation, the entertaining animation and beautiful CG work would collapse. As the story evolves, the house takes shape and the movie gets closer and closer to its final form."

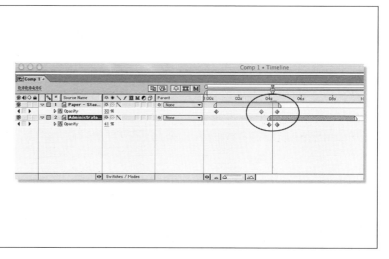

Image Resolution

figure | 9-5 |

Building a story reel using
After Effects.

PRIME TIME AND SATURDAY MORNING ANIMATION

Storyboard artists for feature animation usually have a year or more to work out story ideas; not so for prime time animation story artists. A typical thirty-minute episode takes about nine months to produce, with a four to six week window allocated to storyboarding. The story artist's role is strictly to tell a story through staging: wide shots to open each new scene, medium shots to showcase a group of characters or movement, and close-ups when characters speak. However, many animated shows go beyond the basic formula of staging by mirroring movie techniques such as showcasing dynamic camera angles and movement. Just watch any episode of *The Simpsons,* and you will see dynamic camera placement.

Although Saturday morning cartoons follow the same structure for storyboarding a show, there is not the same emphasis on moving beyond the basic formula. The reason is money. Saturday morning cartoons are usually syndicated shows, which means that the rights to a cartoon will be sold to a television or cable station. If a show is popular, more stations will buy the program, but if it falters, the number of stations that broadcast it will decrease. Prime time animation, on the other hand, is owned by the networks, which have the money to hire many more writers and artists to create quality programming.

figure |9-6|

Animation storyboards often feature dynamic movement to tell the story.

Courtesy of Tom Mahoney

The Making of a Prime Time Animated Short

It takes many people to put together an episode of an animated series such as *The Simpsons* or *King of the Hill*. At one time, there are at least a dozen or more episodes of a show in production, each of which goes through several different departments, from story to layout to music.

The Director

The director oversees the entire production process, from visualizing the story to providing approvals for storyboards, animation, and layout. Most animation directors work on one show at a time and oftentimes contribute to the creation of the storyboards.

The Story Department

The goal of the story department is to bring all the writers together to generate story ideas for new episodes. Once ideas are formulated, each writer gets a shot at writing an outline for an episode. Once the outline is complete, it goes to the staff and together they write the first draft. Rewrites continue as it goes through the table reading process, where the script is read by the writers and ultimately by the voice actors of the characters. Once the script receives final approval, the audio track is recorded.

This process deviates from the creation of feature scripts, which often relies on creating storyboards together with the script. Given such tight schedules with prime time animation, only finalized scripts are given to the storyboard artists.

Storyboards to Animatics

The artists receive the visual parameters for a story from the director along with a rough voice track, which the story artists use as a guide. When the voice track is recorded, the actors may ad-lib jokes, which are rendered out in storyboard form. This happens quite often on an animated show and is something that the writers expect.

A typical half-hour show will average about one thousand panels. Once the panels are approved, each scene is cleaned up and scanned into the computer. Using programs such as Avid, After Effects, or Adobe Premiere, the animator then creates a rough cut from the storyboards. (This process is the same as with feature animation.) To create the story reel, the voice track is "slugged" (timed out) and matched to each panel as it comes up on the screen. Time projections are made for any actions that are nonverbal, such as a character stomping her feet. The storyboard artist will often act out the scenes, timing them with a stopwatch.

Animatic to Screen

Once the animatic is complete, the animators begin to render the final animation. Creating in-betweens (filling in animation between key poses) and cleaning up the animation (pencil lines) is often done in Korea, where it is much cheaper to produce. When the art returns to the United States, more revisions are made before it is edited using the animatic as a template.

Music and sound effects are also added to the final animation. Creating the final animation for most half-hour shows usually takes four to six months (*The Simpsons* takes ten weeks), compared to six weeks for a half-hour live-action show.

> *"The storyboard artist's job is to plan out the entire show, write all the dialogue, and decide the mood, action, jokes, pacing, etc., of every scene. And if the board doesn't work, the show won't work. So what I do is supervise the boarding process trying to get the shows the way I'd like them to be."*
>
> Craig McCracken,
> Creator/Producer
> *The Powerpuff Girls*

figure 9-7

Storyboard from *The Bone Collector.*
Courtesy of Universal Studios

FILM

As mentioned earlier in the chapter, animation storyboards are created in tandem with the script. This process rarely happens with live-action productions, although it is not unheard of. In fact, George Lucas created the script for *Star Wars: The Phantom Menace* along with the storyboards. However with most films, the director receives the finalized script before the storyboard process begins. The director is responsible for analyzing the screenplay in terms of character development, conflict, and its tone and pace. Many directors will block the action and special effects sequences of a production. This includes how the characters move within a scene in relation to the camera. Many directors, however, go beyond the scope of storyboarding only special effects and action sequences. One of the first motion pictures to storyboard the majority of its sequences was Steven Spielberg's *Raiders of the Lost Ark*. The film was storyboarded months in advance, which gave the crew a grasp of what to expect from equipment to costumes changes for the various scenes.

Many directors, like Spielberg, use storyboard artists to translate their vision by breaking down the script into shot-by-shot sketches from the point of view of the camera. M. Night Shyamalan, director of *The Sixth Sense* and *Signs*, first lays out the entire picture in his imagination before committing any ideas to paper. For the film *Signs*, Shyamalan spent several months creating storyboards for every single scene in the movie. He then paired the storyboard drawings to the script. By the time the crew was ready to shoot, he had the entire picture edited on paper.

Akira Kurosawa, the famed director of such films as *Ran*, *The Seven Samurai*, and *Rashomon*, staged his films by creating elaborate storyboards, which he painted himself. His storyboards depicted beautifully choreographed shots and vivid color in which he naturally drew the audience's attention to the most important elements.

Most production storyboards, however, are not as elaborate as Kurosawa's. Many, in fact, are no more than stick figures or rough sketches. Ridley Scott, director of *Gladiator* and *Black Hawk Down*, was a film student when he started creating his own storyboards. The first sketches he produced were for *Alien*. The drawings were no more than thumbnail drawings drawn on the back of the script and referred to by his crew as "Ridleygrams." The producers were so impressed with Scott's sketches that the studio rewarded him by doubling the film's budget.

Action and Special Effect Sequences

Let's say you are asked to storyboard a scene of a car weaving in and out of traffic when suddenly it jumps the median, lands in front of an eighteen-wheeler, and explodes.

Scenes similar to the exploding car are difficult to express, especially if you do not provide visual cues. An overhead diagram and storyboards will assist the production team in planning where the camera should be positioned and at what distance. Diagrams and storyboards also outline potential problems.

Storyboards are indispensable for complicated action and special effects sequences that have never been tried before, especially when it comes to gunfire, explosions, and car chases. It is much better to experiment on paper—where mistakes can be made—than with a camera and special effects crew.

Another reason for preplanning action sequences is consistency. If a scene is extremely complicated, there may be a second or third film unit working on various shots. With the aid of storyboards, each unit can match the "look" of the other shots within a scene.

> *"When it comes to stunts or special effects, they should be planned like an army maneuver."*
>
> Gillian Armstrong, Director
> *Oscar and Lucinda*

TIP

To gain a wider understanding of timing, watch movies, or more specifically action sequences. For example, set the counter on your DVD player to see how long a chase sequence lasts.

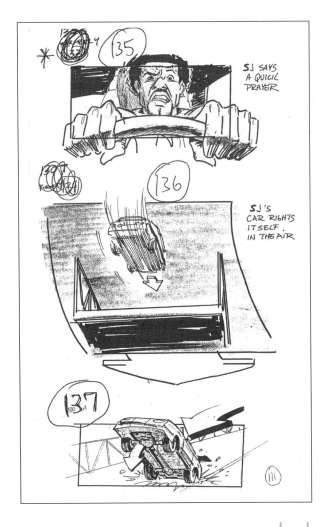

figure **9-8**

Storyboard from *2 Fast 2 Furious.*
Courtesy of Universal Studios

Storyboards are also used as a starting point for planning visual effects that rely heavily on computer graphics. During the preproduction phase, the storyboard artist may sketch digital characters, miniatures, and environments. It is in the storyboard phase that characters and environments will be refined, before actual modeling takes place. By refining drawings, the visual effects team can foresee if a shot is possible, and how it will unfold. An example is *The Perfect Storm*, directed by Wolfgang Petersen. Petersen, along with the visual effects supervisor and cinematographer, met with storyboard artists to convey their ideas for how to shoot a violent ocean storm. They discussed the direction the ship should be pointed in, the height of the waves, and strength of the winds. The storyboard artists then sketched the scene based on these meetings. Once Petersen approved the storyboards, the visual effects team created animatics before actual production started. Such complex scenes may go through several revisions in the preproduction phase before being given final approval.

Many action and special effects storyboards use the edges of the frame of the storyboard panel. This is sometimes done to convey the fluid action that takes place outside of the frame, as well as what is in it. Remember, what is left out of a frame is just as important.

MUSIC VIDEOS

Music videos are about image and creating hype around an artist or band to help promote album sales. Record companies pick the song they believe will be the big hit on the record charts. Once the single for the album is chosen, the record label accepts bids from several directors for the job. The directors involved in the bid receive job parameters, which may include information such as the song lyrics and rhythm. Potential directors then go off and create storyboards from this information, which will ultimately be presented to the record company executives.

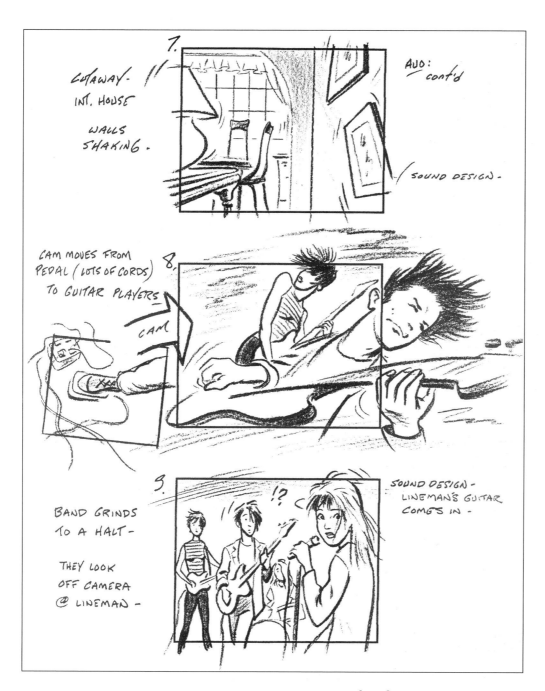

As storyboards are created, directors must keep in mind that most music videos rarely follow a narrative structure. Many music videos employ jump cuts, montage sequences, and dynamic transitions, such as the quick cut, wipe, and dissolve. Music videos also employ dynamic camera movement, such as dollies, pans, and tilt shots.

figure **9-9**

Production storyboard.
Artist: Matt Karol
Courtesy of Washington Square Arts & Film

CHAPTER SUMMARY

Each scene within an animated production is storyboarded according to the vision of the animation director. In feature animation, the story artist works alongside the writers of a screenplay to flesh out story ideas, illuminating its characters, locations, jokes, and mood. The storyboard artist may go back and forth a number of times with the director or writers of a production until they feel the idea is solid. Animation storyboards for television, on the other hand, are specifically created to show the staging of a scene. The storyboard artist is usually provided with a rough voice track for assistance with shot composition. Once storyboards are complete, they are scanned into the computer and slugged to a dialogue track.

Many film productions storyboard the special effects and complex action sequences. This is extremely important to a production for a number of reasons. One, it allows the director to experiment on paper, which is much cheaper than during production. Two, storyboards allow for consistency when there are many crew members working on a scene. Three, it allows the director to see if certain visual effects are even possible.

Often music videos do not follow a narrative flow. Many are made up of montage sequences that consist of jump cuts and dramatic transitions and camera angles.

in review

1. What is the difference between animation and live-action storyboards?

2. What is the average schedule for storyboarding an animated television episode?

3. What are story reels?

4. How does the storyboard help the producer of an animated television show?

5. How does the job of the storyboard artist differ between television and feature animation?

6. Why are backgrounds only created for each new scene for animation storyboards?

7. Name two reasons why film directors storyboard special effects and action scenes.

8. What film directors rely heavily on the use of storyboards for their productions?

9. How do music videos differ from film when it comes to the storyboard process?

exercises

1. Develop a shot list and animation storyboard for the following scene:

   What appears to be an oversized soup can with a dome lid hurtles through space, twisting and turning every which way down to Earth. It skims across the treetops, around bridges and buildings, whipping into the air anything not anchored down. The ship guides its way to an open field for an emergency landing. As the ship gets closer, a house and barn come into view. The ship attempts to land in the field, showering ears of corn onto the landscape. The ship slows its destructive path, but not soon enough. BOOM! The ship crashes through the upstairs window of the house and whizzes out the back door, crashing through the barn, and stopping in a haystack. The animals in the barn turn to look at the smoldering haystack. As the animals move cautiously toward the object, the haystack RUSTLES, and out pops EDDIE the warthog, wearing a bomber jacket, goggles, and helmet.

2. Write a short action scene that features a car chase and several explosions. Next, create the shot list and storyboards for the scene.

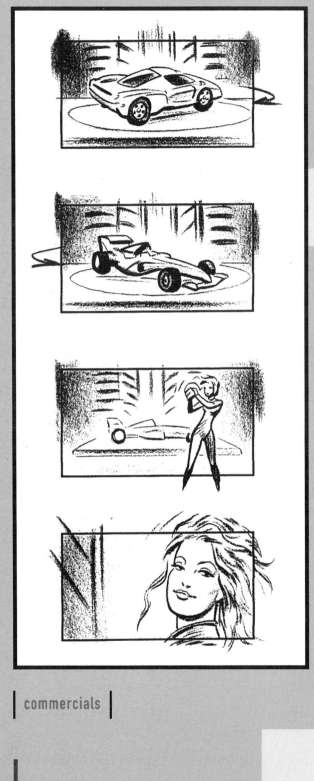

Courtesy of Matt Karol

commercials

objectives

introduction

Advertising is a part of our everyday lives, from broadcast commercial spots to messages sold on our coffee warmers. It also happens to be a multibillion-dollar industry, which translates into an enormous amount of commercials that are produced each year. When it comes to advertising, some of the top spending categories include automotive, retail, financial, and cosmetics. Securing the average thirty-second spot during the Super Bowl costs roughly two million dollars. Big advertisers such as Procter and Gamble, Ford, Budweiser, and Pepsi are willing to spend considerable amounts of money to attract the largest television audience of the entire year. However, it is during the remainder of the year that most companies advertise, with the average cost for commercial time at $350,000, or almost $12,000 per second.

It is the advertising agency's job to come up with ideas that are thought provoking and memorable. If vying for a new account, an advertising agency must be invited by the company to participate in a pitch for a new product. The agency will more than likely compete against several other agencies for a new account. If the agency is pitching a creative strategy for an existing client's product, however, the agency must come up with several ideas for how to execute the new message.

The tool of choice for an agency pitch is the presentation storyboard: highly rendered storyboards that are used to sell an idea to a client. These are much different from production storyboards, which are used as a working blueprint for film, television, or animation.

This chapter explores the process involved in and the people responsible for creating an advertising campaign, from the creative brief to the presentation storyboard to the ripomatic.

figure |10-1|

The average thirty-second commercial that runs during the Super Bowl costs two million dollars.

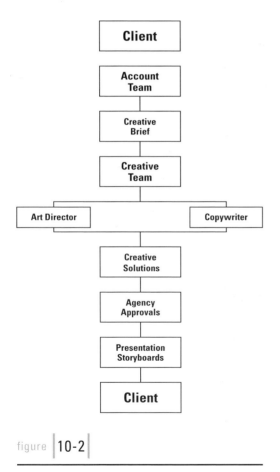

figure |10-2|

Steps to creating presentation storyboards.

THE TEAM

The team that produces the creative strategy for an advertising campaign begins with the account manager and creative director, and ultimately ends up in the hands of the art director and copywriter, who are responsible for shaping the message.

Account Manager

The account manager, also known as the account executive, is the contact person between the agency and the client. It is the account manager's job to understand the client's needs and handle all requests. The account manager is a problem solver, in addition to a creative thinker who shapes the ideas for a product or service in the form of a strategy.

Creative Director

The creative director is responsible for overseeing the creative team. The creative director supervises the development of the creative concept and the look and feel of the composition and design for a product or service.

Art Director

The art director is responsible for visualizing and ultimately executing the creative ideas for a new product or service. The art director should have talent in many areas, including illustration, concept development, layout, and even copywriting. The art director is also in charge of overseeing the creation of the storyboards, which are considerably detailed compared to production storyboards for film and animation.

Copywriter

The copywriter is a wordsmith who must study the creative strategy and the facts before disseminating the message. Whereas the art director uses visuals to persuade an individual to buy a product or service, the copywriter uses words. The copywriter often works directly with the art director, brainstorming ideas for attention-getting ideas.

THE CREATIVE PROCESS

Many of us have fallen victim to an advertising message that touts products such as fast food, cleaning products, or services for a financial advisor. If you are a chocolate fanatic, for instance, it may be hard to resist warm, milk chocolate being drizzled atop creamy, caramel nougat as the slogan hypes "It's good to be bad." The advertiser has done a good job if you come home one afternoon with several of those same candy bars in hand.

Whether the advertiser is selling candy or cars, the creative process involves the production of ideas that are conveyed with both words and pictures. This begins with the creative team translating the advertising brief into the creative concept.

"The secret of all effective originality in advertising is not the creation of new and tricky words and pictures, but one of putting familiar words and pictures into new relationships."

Leo Burnett, Agency Owner

figure **10-3**

Key frame from storyboard for Samsung.

Artist: Don Anderson

Courtesy of e2amp, inc.

The Creative Brief

With the high cost of ads and only thirty seconds to get a message across to audiences, the visuals and the message must be well planned out. The first step in the process has nothing to do with the actual creation of the visuals and everything to do with understanding the client's needs. This begins with the creative brief that answers who, what, where, and when. The *who* of the brief are those individuals exposed to the advertising message—the target audience. *What* are the product's features and benefits, and the expected tone of the commercial spot (how you want the message to sound). The *where* is the media in which the ads will play.

The brief motivates the creative team to generate ideas that describe the overall approach for creating the advertising campaign. It is their goal to come up with a creative concept that is both original and that dramatizes the selling message to prospective customers.

Target Audience

The group to whom you want to advertise a client's products is called the target audience. This group usually includes both a primary and secondary audience. Individuals who make up the primary audience will be directly affected by the client's message. Variables of a primary target audience include household income, education, gender, aspirations, culture, and so forth.

People within the secondary audience are of lesser importance to receive a client's message. Although they are not the main focus, the secondary audience still benefit from the message.

Target Audience

The new PC notebook is designed for professionals on the move. The individuals who use the new PC notebook require a system that is lightweight and portable for all their business and personal needs.

figure 10-4

Example of target audience description.

One of the most important elements for the creative team is an individual's attitudes and beliefs, or what the individual feels about a product. It is here that the spark for the creative campaign begins.

Tone

The tone or mood of an advertisement is crucial to conveying the benefits of a product or service. Whether you are selling deodorants, financial services, fragrances, or allergy medication, emotional triggers are used. The visuals of an advertisement work in tandem with

figure | 10-5 |

Speed Stick shooting storyboard.

Artist: Matt Karol

Courtesy of Octane Films

the message to create ads that are funny, warm, passionate, or authoritative. Take, for instance, a skin care commercial that displays radiant women with the appearance of smooth, ageless skin. The tone is light as the women laugh and smile. The message: *If you buy our skin cream, you too can look radiant and ageless.* By using emotional triggers, the advertisers are not selling just a skin care product, but also happiness and youth. The goal of the art director and copywriter is to reach a product's target audience at an emotional level to build and reinforce brand loyalty, to satisfy needs, or to solve their problem better than the competition. The "Just Do It" Nike campaign, for instance, evokes feelings of accomplishment, whereas Alka Seltzer's "I can't believe I ate the whole thing" campaign satisfies the problem of indigestion.

Features, Benefits, and Visual Imagery

The more specific the advertising message, the more effective the results. When interpreting the message through visuals, it is necessary that the advertisement demonstrate the features and benefits of a product or service.

Features include what a product looks, smells, feels, and tastes like. For example, features of the Volkswagen Bug include power windows, folding rear seats, leather upholstery, and much more.

 The average person is exposed to about 3,000 ads each day.

Benefits on the other hand, are how a product makes consumers feel, or more specifically what it can do for them. Using the Volkswagen example, the benefits to consumers may be that it makes audiences feel young and cool, saves money on gas, or that it is just a fun car to drive.

figure 10-6

Advertising appeals are aimed at influencing our attitudes toward a wide range of consumer products and behaviors.

ADVERTISING APPEALS	
Health	Appeals to body-conscious people or health seekers
Love	Used to sell cosmetics or perfume
Fear	Social embarrassment, old age, loss of health
Convenience	Used to sell fast foods
Admiration	Use of a celebrity spokesperson
Fun/Pleasure	Used to advertise beer, vacations, parks
Vanity	Used for expensive items
Environment	Centers on environmental protection

At the center of the commercial message is the product, which advertisers try to coax consumers to buy because of its unique benefits.

A strong link must be created between the message and the benefits to the consumer. A Mountain Dew commercial from several years back, for instance, uses engaging visual imagery to sell its message. The spot showcases a couple snowboarding off a cliff with parachutes. In midair the guy pulls out a Mountain Dew and two straws. The girl accepts the soda then pulls the guy's ripcord and keeps the Dew. By creating strong visual imagery, the advertiser sells the idea to consumers that if they drink Mountain Dew, they too are risk takers and individuals that live life to the fullest.

IMPLEMENTATION OF THE IDEA

An advertising campaign is created in two parts: the script and the storyboard.

A commercial script contains scenes and shots, just as with film or animation. However, where scenes are numerous in film, the average number of scenes for a thirty-second commercial spot is about four to six. The storyboard illustrates only the key frames for each scene, with the dialogue written underneath each frame.

| TIP |

Unusual camera angles often work to grab the viewer's attention.

figure | 10-7 |

Selected key frames.
Courtesy of Henry Alfonzo

The Script

It is the role of the copywriter to translate the creative brief into an actual script for a commercial spot. With only thirty seconds to get the message across to the target audience, television copy should be succinct and kept to one specific idea. Remember, at the heart of the story line is the product. The copywriter makes sure the script explains the visuals, to draw the audience into the message. For example, two hot, steaming pizzas fill the screen as the narrator declares "two pizzas for the price of one" in the Little Caesars commercials.

The copywriter needs to consider the following when developing the product's message:

- What is the purpose for the product or service?
- How is the product or service better than its competitors?
- How much does the product cost?

The Storyboard

The art director is the individual responsible for the execution of an advertising campaign strategy, ensuring that it is both visually appealing and unique to its target audience. The art director will either create the presentation storyboards or provide guidance to an artist who actually illustrates them.

figure |10-8|

Health club commercial.
Courtesy of Juan Plaza

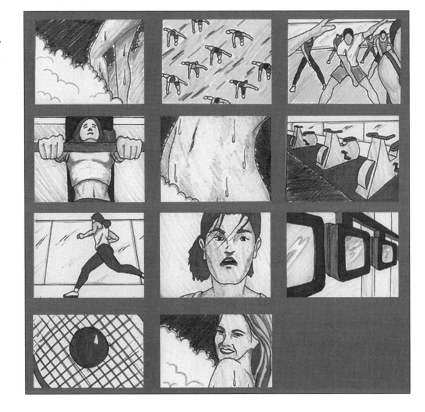

Since the purpose of the presentation storyboard is to sell an idea, the storyboard artist needs to pay particularly close attention to details such as clothing, facial expressions, and, of course, product identification, which is always at the center of the advertising message.

If the visuals do not catch the eye of the audience in the first three seconds, chances are they are going to change the channel.

From Pencil Sketch to Final Illustrations

Rendering commercial storyboards begins with pencil sketches and ends with highly detailed illustrations.

The artist begins a storyboard job once the art director provides rough thumbnails, which exhibit the mood and look for a commercial. Using the thumbnails as a guide, the artist creates pencil sketches, which are created fast and loose to establish the composition of a shot. Once pencil sketches are complete, they are usually submitted to the art director for approval. At this stage in the process, it is quite simple for an artist to make any necessary changes. Once approved, the drawings are inked for contrast. Inking is an important step because it adds depth to the image. It is also important for photocopying purposes since pencil is hard to pick up.

figure 10-9

Pencil sketch.
Courtesy of Matt Karol

After sketches are inked, they are usually rendered with color markers. This, however, depends on the needs of the client. If markers are used, it is important to consider how colors interact with each other so that continuity is maintained and meaning is created. That means understanding the difference between warm and cool colors, contrasting colors, and how colors blend together.

figure | 10-10 |

Presentation storyboard.
Courtesy of Kunthearo Veun

| TIP |

Commercial storyboards should always be photocopied before they are mounted, in case the client asks for a copy.

Storyboard Format

Panels for commercial storyboards are created in a format that is manageable, yet adequate for presentation purposes. In most cases, panels are rendered for a 1.33:1 aspect ratio, although with the rise of widescreen television we will surely see this change. Popular panel sizes amongst artists are 3 x 5 and 5 x 7 inches. Storyboard artists, however, should feel comfortable working in all different sizes. Once panels are fully rendered, they are mounted for presentation purposes.

The Shooting Board

Once the presentation storyboard is approved, the final stage is to create the shooting storyboard, which is used during the actual production of the commercial. The agency hires a director who is responsible for the final product. The director may use the illustrations from the presentation storyboard in the development of the shooting board. The shooting board is filled out with many more illustrations that are necessary to tell the story. A fast-paced commercial may have twenty to thirty shots, whereas a slower-paced commercial may have only a handful. It is the director's job to make sure pacing is consistent with the message.

Similar to film and animation, the commercial shooting board includes technical information, such as camera angles and movement, and is used to guide the team during production.

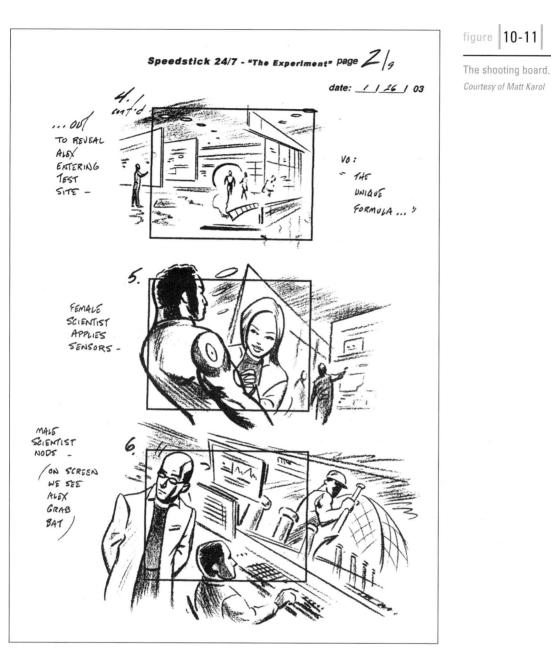

figure 10-11

The shooting board.
Courtesy of Matt Karol

The Ripomatic

Animatics play an important role in the creation of advertising campaigns and are often created by the agency for presentation to the client before shooting begins. Ad agency animatics are often called *ripomatics*, which are storyboards spliced together with images from other commercials. Ripomatics may also be used in focus groups to get audience reaction to the advertising spot. Animatics will be discussed further in Chapter 13.

THE STORYBOARD ARTIST
AT WORK

Don Anderson

Q. What was your first storyboard job?

A. When I left school I got a job working on a small, horror movie starring Drew Barrymore. I was originally brought on to work on black-and-white storyboards, but the job changed to doing nine full-color presentation boards. I had six days to work, at $100 a day, and there were several problems. I hadn't done large-scale color pieces before, I was inexperienced with perspective, I didn't know how to pace myself yet, and worst of all, I was too scared to ask questions that would have cleared a lot of things up.

It was Friday, and I had six boards due Monday morning. The rep from the agency was gone for the weekend, and I didn't know what to do. My first big break into storyboards and I felt like a complete failure. Saturday I called one of my teachers. He said that no matter what had happened, I had to get the job done. I had an obligation to finish and he told me to look at some art books, get inspired and just do it. And that's what I did. Monday I arrived to the production office, with all the pieces in hand. The surprised look on the director's face made the weekend of stress and no sleep absolutely worth it.

Later, when I talked to my rep, he said that they knew they were working with someone green, and they should have been more forthright with what they wanted. He's right, but from then on, whenever I worked on a project, I always asked questions if I wasn't clear on something, even if the questions seemed stupid.

Q. What is the process for creating commercial storyboards for clients such as Samsung?

A. Usually what happens is I'll either work on site at an ad agency and meet with the art director, or I'll work out of my studio, and contact will be via phone. They will tell me what they are looking for and sometimes have small thumbnail drawings showing me what they need.

They'll often have the reference I need, or I'll do research on the Web for it. Then I do a quick rough sketch to show the layout of the composition and elements. I either do this on tracing paper in black or on regular copy paper with nonphoto blue pencil. Once the art director approves that, I tighten it up to the final drawing. Again I show it to the art director and make changes if necessary. If I'm not doing the final in color, then I'll work the shading more to give the drawing some substance and weight. If color is asked for, then I'll keep the shading to a minimum and let the color do its work.

I'll either do the color with markers or scan the drawing in and color it in Photoshop. Recently, I've been working more in Photoshop, as it is easier to make changes.

Q. What materials do you use to create presentation storyboards?

A. The materials I use are black Prismacolor pencils (they give you the best darks when you copy them), Faber Castell Pitt Artist pen (Brush pen) or Le Plume for deep flat black areas, and Pentel Milky Gel Roller for whites (if I have a lot of time, I might use white gouache). I've started using Calque tracing paper from Canson, after a friend recommended it to me. It's got a great smooth surface that works great with the black Prismacolor, almost like vellum.

Q. What are the basic skills an individual needs to become a storyboard artist?

A. You need to be able to draw just about anything that you can think of. Drawing people is probably most important, of all ages and ethnicities, from every conceivable angle. Learn perspective and be able to draw objects, cars, and buildings (also from every angle). You need to communicate well and work as part of a team, keeping in mind that you are an extension of someone else's vision, either the director or the art director. And you must do it all as quickly and clearly as humanly possible.

Q. Do you have any advice for students interested in the field of storyboarding?

A. I read in an article, that you need four things to make it in this business: 1) perseverance, 2) networking skills, 3) a good attitude at work (being fun to work with), and 4) talent. And that is the order of importance!

You need *perseverance* to get through all the hungry times and all the people that will tell you that you can't do it. This is about being confident in yourself and your abilities, and having the focus and drive to follow through, no matter what.

You need good *networking skills* because you have to go out and find the people who will give you jobs, since nobody is going to do it for you.

You need to have a *good attitude,* because you are working on high-pressure jobs with stressed out people, and nobody wants to work with a prima donna artist. Some of the "best" artists I've seen aren't working because they can't take criticism or they just think they're above it all.

And *talent* comes last, although I would probably change that to skill instead. Talent sounds like some magical thing that you are born with, but you can learn the drawing skills you need if you want it bad enough (see rule #1). This is about working hard at your craft and drawing every day.

CHAPTER SUMMARY

Presentation storyboards are used to "sell" a campaign strategy to a client. The art director is responsible for turning the creative brief of a product into visuals. The creative brief includes information regarding target audience, features and benefits, and the tone of the message.

There are several team members that plan the advertising campaign: the account manager is the contact person between the agency and the client, the creative director oversees the creative team, the art director visualizes the creative ideas, the storyboard artist executes creative ideas in the form of presentation panels, and the copywriter vocalizes the message.

The process of creating presentation storyboards begins with pencil sketches, which are then inked for contrast. Presentation storyboards are rendered either with color markers or within computer programs such as Photoshop. If the agency wins the bid, a director will be assigned to shoot the commercial. Oftentimes, the director will require shooting boards, which include technical information to guide the team during production.

in review

1. What are the major differences between a commercial storyboard and a production storyboard?

2. Why do pencil sketches need to be inked before they are scanned into the computer?

3. What is the average number of key frames for a thirty-second commercial?

4. Who is responsible for interpreting the creative brief?

5. What are several formats for creating presentation storyboards?

exercises

1. Spend several hours studying television commercials. Answer the following questions as you consider them:

   - What is the commercial trying to sell?

   - What are the features and benefits of the product?

   - What was visually stimulating about the commercial?

   - Who is the target audience?

2. Create your own thirty-second commercial spot for a pizza company. Once you have finished the script, sketch each key frame and render in full color. Mount your work for presentation.

new media

© Cos Russo Dejavu Worlds

objectives

Understand storyboarding for multimedia

Understand the development of storyboard sequences for illustrating navigation
options and the graphic look

Identify elements of the game design document for storyboarding

Learn to use the storyboard as a guide, to help lay out your edit list of "scenes"
in a manageable order

introduction

We are living in an age where the audience is no longer passive, but an active participant in
the dissemination of information. Today there are Internet cafés, cell phones that make it
possible to check email and take pictures, Web sites that allow us to download music or
movies, and e-commerce sites where we can buy practically anything from plane tickets to real
estate. The possibilities are endless.

We often think about things that are interactive as any combination of animation, text, graphics,
sound, and video that is controlled by the user within a computer environment. When a user
clicks a button, for instance, an application might forward to a video sequence or to the next
screen. The user controls where to go within the program and the speed at which the
information is viewed. But sometimes more interaction comes from the program. Think of it this
way: when a user plays a computer game that gets harder as the player scores more points, in
essence, the computer game acts as another player would, and in this case, the difficulty level
is modified according to points scored by the player.

Interactive programs act as a road map with many possible paths to choose from. If it is a
game, you might acquire points for taking the shortest route, or simply obtain information that
may lead to new levels and special features. If doing research on the Internet, you may narrow
your search by using a search engine. From the results, you pick and choose the links with the
highest relevancy to the topic.

But where do storyboards fit into the realm of interactive games or Web sites? Ask almost any
designer—whether they are designing games or information kiosks—and they will most likely
tell you that storyboards help the entire team to map out how ideas will look and work. As a
designer of informational CD-ROMs and educational games, outlining each screen was
absolutely vital to my job. By storyboarding my own projects, I was able to see not only what a
project would look like, but also how it would function. By using storyboards, I organized all the

elements, such as navigational choices, graphics, and animation, which assisted both the creative and technical teams during production.

As you move through this chapter, you will learn where storyboards fit into the overall scheme for creating interactive products. This includes the role of key players, the creation of the design document, and the conception of Cinematics, or full-motion video sequences.

figure | 11-1a |

Game Web site where kids play back different sounds in a desired sequence for the Willy Wonka Candy Web site.

Artist: Don Anderson

Courtesy of wonka.com

figure | 11-1b |

Oompas Wild Rush. Illustration, animation, and game design for Willy Wonka Candy Web site game.

Artist: Don Anderson

Courtesy of wonka.com

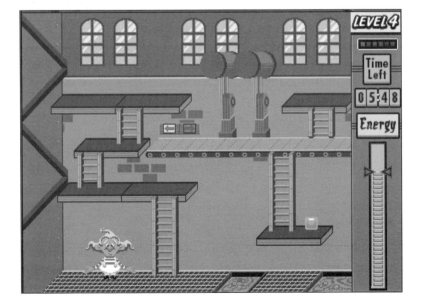

THE TEAM

Many of today's e-commerce sites, computer games, and interactive training programs have large teams of people working on them. What that means is that everyone must be on the same page if they are to produce a successful product. Understanding the roles of the creative team can add to the success of the individual who is creating the project storyboards.

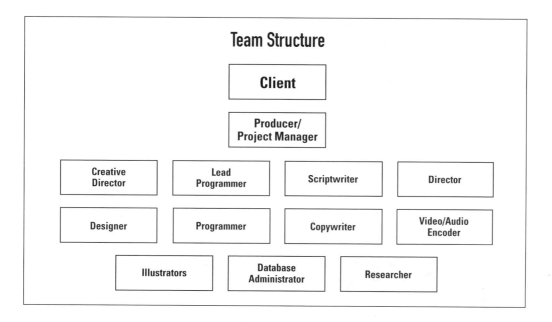

The Creative Director

The creative director (sometimes it will be the art director) oversees the creative team and is responsible for the output of visuals, which includes managing the creation of interface screens, animation, full-motion video, and sound. The creative director must communicate ideas to team members such as programmers, scriptwriters, graphic artists, and designers. One way to communicate ideas is with the storyboard, which determines the logical flow and look of an interactive application.

The Designer

The designer is responsible for conceptualizing the elements of an interactive product to make for an exciting experience for the end user. If the product is a strategy game, for instance, the designer must create a world in which the game takes place, the rules of game play, several levels of obstacles and challenges, and the look and feel of the game.

figure | 11-2 |

Possible roles for a midsize project.

The lead designer of an interactive application almost always creates the storyboards. They are created very early in the process as a guide for how a project will look, as well as how a user will interact with it. The designer storyboards both the structure and content of each screen, which may include the arrangement of graphics, sound, animation, video, and navigational buttons.

The Producer

The producer, who is usually one of the first individuals assigned to a project, oversees the technical and creative teams. The producer drives the production by handling such things as the budget, project strategy, and schedules. If the budget for a project is relatively small, the producer might lend a hand in design documentation, which includes both flowcharts and storyboards.

The Writer

The writer of interactive programs must have a full understanding for how such programs are constructed. Writers must value not only the storytelling process, but the design process as well. When developing an interactive script, the writer must put the user's experience first. Texts are created that may be altered by both its content and the way it is presented.

The Programmer

The programmer is the individual responsible for writing the code and creating the authoring environment that ties together the content, artwork, and navigational choices. There must be a strong relationship between the programmer and the design team, to understand what will work within the authoring environment.

The Director

Many games, training programs, and informational Web sites include full-motion video sequences. If video is not acquired through a client, then an outside director may be hired to develop video sequences for the project.

TARGET AUDIENCE

Projects are designed for a specific audience, which is one of the most important factors when planning a project. The content and complexity of a game, for instance, will vary greatly if it is targeted to preschoolers versus early teens. If you were creating a Web site on cooking the perfect Thanksgiving turkey, your target audience may include both experienced and inexperienced cooks. Researching your audience will help you determine the project's style, complexity of navigational choices, and content.

PROJECT GOALS AND OBJECTIVES

The first step for the designer is to determine the project goals—whether it will be to entertain, inform, or educate. Goals should be conceived early in the process; this sets the tone for everything else to follow. Setting realistic goals will assist the producer in keeping with project milestones, in addition to visualizing the storyboards. For instance, a goal may be to create an informational CD-ROM on Mexican architecture. Objectives, on the other hand, are a bit more specific. An objective may be to improve instruction by offering historical lessons on Mexican architecture, by integrating content, photo exhibits, and a question and answer section. Clarifying objectives aids the creative team with the mood and style of the project.

Every project has different goals and objectives, whether it is a role-playing game, informational kiosk, or e-commerce site. Several questions to consider when determining project goals and objectives include:

- Why are you developing this project?
- What are your primary goals for the project?
- Does this particular idea merit an interactive form?
- What interactive features might enhance the program?
- Can the content be transferred easily to other platforms?
- What current programs compete with this one?
- How do I want my target audience to feel while navigating through the program?

▶ CASE STUDY: THE MAKING OF ALIDA

Alida is a first-person, point-and-click adventure game in the vein of *Riven* and *Myst,* created by Dejavu Worlds. Cos Russo, the game's creator, wanted to produce an experience that went beyond being just a computer game. As soon as he came up with the idea of a giant guitar as the game's environment, he knew there was no turning back.

figure |11-3|

3D animated game *Alida*.
© Cos Russo
Dejavu Worlds

The Concept

Alida is set on an island of the same name where a rock band has built a theme park, which resembles a mega-size guitar. Troubles split the band up, which puts a halt to its construction. As time passes, the four members of the band each stake a claim to part of the island. When relations between the former band members become even more strained, they lock away the remainder of their fortune in a central vault until legal matters are resolved. Years pass, and then their former manager Kivas tries to get the band together again on the island. Band member Arin, who went to Alida ten days before, hasn't been heard from since. His wife Julia sends the game player to find Arin and bring him home.

It took game designer Cos Russo several revisions to establish the concept and objectives, which are to find Arin, thwart the corrupted members of his former band, and unravel an odd mystery that unfolds during the game.

figure |11-4|

3D animated game *Alida*.
© Cos Russo
Dejavu Worlds

CASE STUDY: THE MAKING OF ALIDA

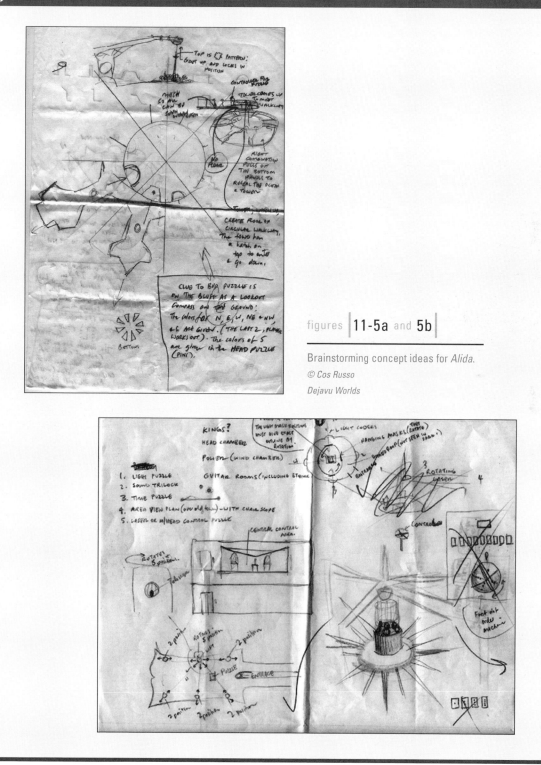

figures | 11-5a and 5b |

Brainstorming concept ideas for *Alida*.

© *Cos Russo*

Dejavu Worlds

CASE STUDY: THE MAKING OF ALIDA

The Script

The game includes video sequences that divulge information about the story, including the estrangement of the band members and their peculiar behavior over the years. Each of these script sequences set the stage, revealing the game's fantasy world told from the perspective of one of the game's characters. The script sequences in *Alida* also sets up game play with intriguing situations that tempt the user to keep playing.

Game Play

Game play is one criterion that is particularly important when creating a game. For *Alida*, game play is centered on the game's puzzles, which are integrated into the game's environment. The goal for *Alida* was to create puzzles that spanned several difficulty levels and that made sense within the story. All the puzzles give a definite response when the player is successful. For example, if the player flips the right switch, it could unlock a door to another part of the island.

figure 11-6

Alida script.

Creation of the Flowchart and Storyboards

The flowchart for *Alida* was fixed from a very early point. The goal was to have many puzzles that ranged from simple to complex. Following the flowchart, sketches of the interfaces, environments, and workings of the puzzles were created to test the waters before Russo took the next step in developing the prototype for the game. The storyboards and flowchart included the following details:

- How the separate environments relate to each character

- The flow from one related puzzle to another

- At what point characters appear during game play

- The placement of clues for the player

CASE STUDY: THE MAKING OF ALIDA

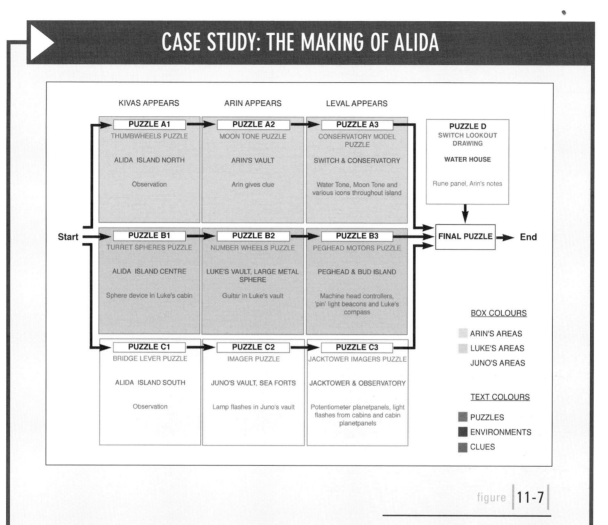

figure | 11-7 |

Alida flowchart.

Production

Game designer Cos Russo wanted the environments of *Alida* to look as real as possible so he photographed parts of Bowral, Australia, which he used to create three-dimensional surface maps. Adobe Photoshop was used extensively, from adjusting the surface maps, to enhancing the final images. Adobe Illustrator was used for all intricate artwork, especially for creating the surface maps. One of the tricky aspects of *Alida* was designing the full-screen animations. The longer animations go from one location to another in what seems to be a single computer, three-dimensional world. In actuality, the animations pass through two or three separate models, which were rendered using Strata Studio Pro, then married together using Final Cut Pro. The final touch was an original music score, which is a powerful tool for setting the right mood, and transporting the player from their environment into the world of *Alida*.

STORYTELLING

Interactive program scripting includes elements of the film script such as plot, location, and well-developed characters. But unlike their film and television counterparts, interactive scripts do not follow a mandatory format. Writers of interactive scenes and stories use whatever format works best for them. Remember, writers who develop multimedia stories are not writing linear stories, but rather interactive stories where the user decides how to navigate through it.

figure | 11-8 |

Example of *Alida* game script.
© Cos Russo
Dejavu Worlds

Storytelling is particularly important to the success of a game project. Games that are high on story content are role-playing, strategy, and adventure games. When the writer develops a game script, how users interact with the game is taken into account. Game story lines may have alternative endings or play selective scenes, depending on the user's skill level. The writer of such scripts must think of all the possible situations and scenarios. Action games, for instance, may offer several options for a user to explore within the game world. The story is told in bits and pieces, and at each level of the game, more of the story is revealed to the user.

To write an interactive story, the scriptwriter needs to use a format that takes into consideration all the levels of a program, which includes visuals and interactivity for each script segment.

THE IMPORTANCE OF DESIGN

The design phase is a necessary step in the organization of a project, and includes the creation of the design document, storyboards, and screen mockups. In this phase, the team determines what ideas may work given the audience, the usability of the product, and how that information is delivered.

The Design Document

The project team collaborates on the design document, which is a description of the entire project with all the details on how the project will be implemented. This document is absolutely critical to the success of the project. When working as a designer, I created meticulous design documents that kept the creative and technical teams abreast of what we were doing. This included project milestones, production elements, description of the design, and interactivity for each interface. By creating the design document, I assured the programmers and artists that what I envisioned was actually feasible within the time constraints and budget projected for the project.

There are many elements that are included within the design document, which may vary in complexity from project to project. Games that are quite complex, for instance, have much more detail than a simple Web site. The basic elements included in a design document are the flowchart, storyboards, design structure, navigation, and character descriptions.

> "When there are a huge number of art assets involved, you absolutely must do concept sketches, story-boards, and anything else you can to reduce risk and any chance of doing stuff over and over again. Poor planning will frustrate people and de-motivate them, so storyboarding is a great way to communicate the overall plan, look and feel, style, and scope of the game."
>
> Chris Taylor
> *Total Annihilation*

Project Structure

How will an interactive project be structured? Once the designer has brainstormed ideas with team members and clarified the objectives, it is time to organize the content. Whether it is a Web site or educational program, the structure must be easy to navigate, offer content that is intriguing, and inspire the user to come back again.

If the interactive Web site is about nutrition, for instance, categories might include dietary guidelines, the food pyramid, nutrition and fitness, and a question and answer section. When designing the structure of a site, you want to make sure that the user can always get back to the home page in two or three clicks. Let's look at the nutrition Web site example.

I. Home Page
II. Dietary Guidelines
    a. The Food Pyramid
        i. Vegetable Group
        ii. Dairy Group
        iii. Meat Group
        iv. Fats, Oils, and Sweets
    b. Nutrition and Fitness
        i. Diet
        ii. Vitamins
        iii. Aerobics
        iv. Recipes
    c. Ask the Doctor
        i. Question and Answer

It is not unusual for a project's structure to be revised several times before the design is final; this is especially true if there is a client involved. Therefore, it is much better to revise the structure of a project within the design document than in the production phase, when interfaces and media are already created.

Flowchart

Just as the director of a film would not show up to a shoot without a written shot list or script breakdown, the designer should never jump into a multimedia project without any documentation for how the application functions. One of the most important documents in the preplanning stage is the flowchart, which visually organizes project information. Once content is structured into categories, the designer assembles the flowchart, which demonstrates a hierarchy of topics in a well-defined layout. In the nutrition example, the home page would be at the top of the hierarchy, with subtopics such as fitness, diet, and the food pyramid at the next level down. The flowchart shows each of the levels by showcasing how screens are linked together.

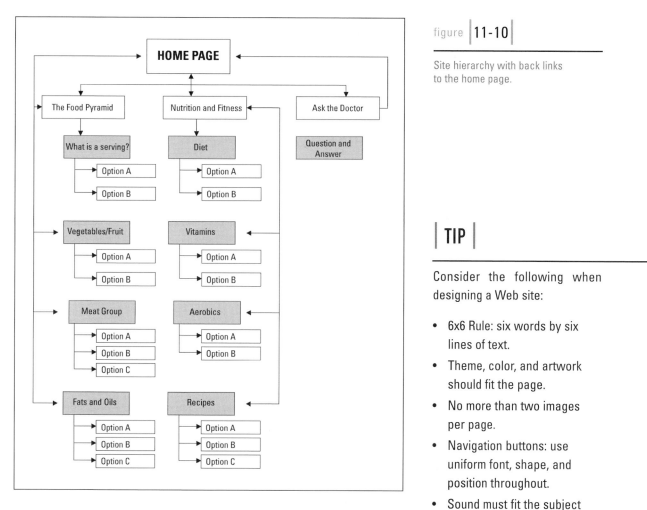

figure | 11-10 |

Site hierarchy with back links
to the home page.

| TIP |

Consider the following when designing a Web site:

- 6x6 Rule: six words by six lines of text.
- Theme, color, and artwork should fit the page.
- No more than two images per page.
- Navigation buttons: use uniform font, shape, and position throughout.
- Sound must fit the subject and tone of a project.
- Three clicks away from the home page.

The number of levels depends on the breadth of information, project goals and objectives, and budget. For example, a topic such as nutrition might only be a few levels deep, whereas a complex game may have twenty different levels and options for the user to choose from. In the latter example, if game play calls for the user to choose from several different doors, each door will lead the user down a different path. At each level, the user may have to overcome several obstacles to get to the next level. All levels, and the paths available, are visualized in the flowchart.

THE STORYBOARD ARTIST AT WORK

Murray Taylor

Murray Taylor, Studio Head, Atari, Inc.

Q. What got you interested in game design?

A. I was in college when the Macintosh was just coming out and I was intrigued by how it was geared specifically to creative people. At about the same time the movie *Tron* was released and after seeing it I thought computer graphics were going to be something I'd like to be involved with. Playing Atari games, coin-op games, and seeing how they were evolving made me realize that it was going to keep getting better and better.

Q. Where do your ideas come from?

A. I get inspiration from many places. N.C. Wyeth's illustrations for *Treasure Island* inspired me for the game *Pirates*! Also lighting in movies will inspire me. Lighting can play a huge part in how a game comes across. Two really different, but equally well-lit movies that I have studied are *Blade Runner* and *Casper*.

Q. As games are getting increasingly complex, many gaming studios are employing the use of animatics. How does your studio use animatics?

A. I am a big proponent for using animatics for game development. They give us a feel for pacing and timing very quickly. We try to get a rough animatic done in a few days and then evaluate it. Someone with a good eye can tell pretty quickly if an idea that sounded good on paper is going to look just as good and tell the story visually. After the initial viewing, we will make timing changes and fine-tune the animatic for a few more days. We can then use that animatic in the game as placeholder art. We do quick sketches, some fast 3D modeling and rendering, as well as scanning images from wherever we can find them. We then put the artwork and animation into Adobe Premiere or After Effects and render out as an AVI file.

Q. How long does it take to design a game from initial concept to production?

A. The game we just finished is *Dungeons and Dragons Heroes.* The design for this type of game takes months, and there are always design issues that come up as the game is being developed. It's pretty typical for a full design to take two to four months.

Q. In your opinion, what makes a really good game designer?

A. I think good game designers tend to have a wide variety of interests and it seems that history is an interest that they have in common. I worked with Sid Meier for many years and he has a keen interest in music and history coupled with a real knack for getting at what's fun and what's not.

Q. Do you storyboard game structure?

A. We use storyboards as flowcharts for all of the decisions that the player could make, up to game play and sometimes into game play. So, if your main menu had three choices, then we would have a mockup of that screen with lines leading to three more mocks of screens representing those choices. And those three screens would lead to others until you reach a screen representing the game. Sometimes the game will have many screens.

Storyboards

The storyboard is a key design document that the entire production team uses as a base for developing an interactive program. Think of the storyboard as a more detailed flowchart, which outlines a story, the look of the interfaces, and how they will function, along with how a user might interact with the content. Storyboards are useful to the development team in defining and grouping elements such as graphics, animation, video, and illustrations. For example, storyboards aid the designer to determine the best media for emphasizing an emotion or story point. Photos, for instance, may work best in revealing a historical aspect of a story or video for a "how to" section of a CD-ROM.

The person creating the storyboards does not necessarily have to be an artist. In fact, the producer, who may have minimal graphic or artistic skills, is often heavily involved in the production of storyboards. The producer may create the storyboards solely in a word processing program, whereas a designer may start with pencil sketches and graduate to full mockups of each interface within a production. As the program is being developed, the mock screens act as a placeholder until the final art is complete.

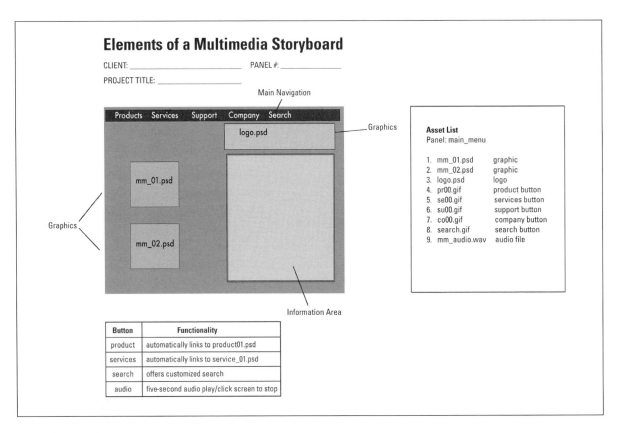

Elements of a Multimedia Storyboard

CLIENT: _____   PANEL #: _____

PROJECT TITLE: _____

Main Navigation

Products   Services   Support   Company   Search

logo.psd — Graphics

mm_01.psd

Graphics

mm_02.psd

Information Area

Asset List
Panel: main_menu

1.	mm_01.psd	graphic
2.	mm_02.psd	graphic
3.	logo.psd	logo
4.	pr00.gif	product button
5.	se00.gif	services button
6.	su00.gif	support button
7.	co00.gif	company button
8.	search.gif	search button
9.	mm_audio.wav	audio file

Button	Functionality
product	automatically links to product01.psd
services	automatically links to service_01.psd
search	offers customized search
audio	five-second audio play/click screen to stop

figure | 11-11 |

Storyboards allow the designer to organize the content and navigational elements in a logical order.

Components of the Interactive Storyboard

Storyboards for games, Web sites, or CD-ROMs are similar to live-action and animation storyboards, yet they also have unique qualities of their own. These include the look and feel of the graphic menus, navigational choices, colors, and what elements, such as video and sound, accompany the interfaces. Each navigational choice specified within the storyboard should support the choices made by the user. Several questions that you should ask include:

- What are the navigational choices from the main interface to other sections of the program?
- What media elements are represented on the main interface?
- What are the main elements on each of the subtopic menus?
- How should elements be arranged?
- What media elements best tell the story for each subtopic?

Suppose a user had to answer ten questions to move up a level in a trivia game, as in figure 11-12a. Each of the ten questions includes four potential answers for the user to choose from. If the user chooses the right answer, the program branches to a video sequence, while choosing any of the three incorrect options forwards the user to a hint screen. Each of these interfaces is storyboarded, including the navigational choices and video sequence.

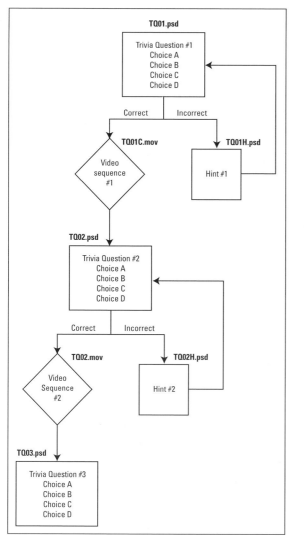

figure **11-12a**

Trivia game flowchart.

figure **11-12b**

A multimedia storyboard shows the affects of each interaction.

Storyboard panels should include file names, which are assigned to each element such as video and animation sequences, as well as a description of where the elements branch to within the application. The designer provides descriptions for each of these elements, either within the margins of the storyboard panel or at the bottom of the page. An asset list (similar to a shot list) should also be generated, to record all the artwork and media elements specified within a program. Asset lists are used for tracking purposes and for assisting the design and technical teams.

The information within the storyboard is often reviewed by the producer of the program or in some cases by the client prior to the start of production.

CINEMATICS

Cinematics, better known as cut scenes, are full-motion video sequences that propel the story line forward by playing video or animation sequences that reflect user selection. Cut scenes often interrupt the interactive sequences of game play, and provide the user with details of the story in a linear structure. Cut scenes often act as the user's "reward" for excelling through several levels of a game.

For instance, if the user defeats the King's Evil Court at level two, a video sequence plays, which not only provides entertainment value, but also reveals information about the characters and story. Cut scenes may also be triggered at the game's introduction, credits, character endings, and game over.

When a game branches to a cut scene, the user is often not in control; they cannot interrupt a cut scene or fast-forward through it. These mandatory cut scenes imitate film, and often comprise a healthy amount of game time. Because of their complexity, cut scenes are almost always storyboarded.

Cut scenes are usually either animation sequences or film sequences of live actors. The problem with most cut scenes is that they oftentimes do not match game play graphics. That is why it is important for the designer, or the person creating the storyboards, to work closely with artists and programmers. This will ensure that the graphic look of the game is translated into the cinematic sequences.

The first step in creating game cinematics is to create the script, which is similar to a film scene. After a cinematic sequence is scripted, the designer works on the storyboards, which map out the action by determining camera framing, camera angles, and movement. Therefore the designer must have a strong knowledge base of camera terminology and techniques to convey the emotion and tension of the story.

If there is time within the schedule and a reasonable budget, cinematic storyboards are often scanned into the computer to create an animatic. The animatic is timed to the narration or audio components and acts as a prototype for the sequence. The production of the animatic helps determine the timing and pacing of a game and ultimately saves the production team time and money.

CHAPTER SUMMARY

Multimedia design can be a time-consuming and complicated process. Storyboards assist the design team with how the end product will look, sound, and function. The lead designer is usually the person who oversees story ideas and the objectives for an application. Once the objectives and target audience are established, the script can be written. Scripts for interactive applications are nonlinear and must be written in bits and pieces. After the script is written, the designer can start working on the flowcharts and storyboards, which represent key content at different stages in the design. Storyboards also provide both the creative and technical teams with information on how each screen will function within the overall scheme of the program.

Cinematics are short, full-motion video or animation sequences that provide the user with details of the story in a linear structure. Storyboards for cinematics follow the same format as production storyboards for film and animation, by highlighting camera framing, camera angles, and movement.

in review

1. What is the difference between multimedia storyboards and production storyboards for film and animation?

2. What is an objective?

3. Who are the primary team members that work on an interactive project?

4. What variables differentiate a target audience?

5. What elements are included in the design document?

6. What is a cut scene?

7. What are the elements in the creation of an interactive storyboard? Why does the designer create a shot list (or asset list) for the storyboard?

8. What is the purpose of the flowchart?

9. What elements need to be considered when brainstorming Web site structure?

10. Who within a production receives a copy of the storyboards?

exercises

1. You just nabbed the job of lead designer for SinLEX Productions. Your job is to oversee the creation of a new Web site for Auto Biz. You have six months to plan and create the site. The areas of the site include car parts, lemon checks, and a sales section. Roughly sketch out a flowchart for Auto Biz, followed by the storyboards. The storyboards should be numbered and reflect screen layout, including navigational choices for the user.

2. Pick your favorite interactive game. Sketch out ten screens from the application. Evaluate the navigation, screen layout, and theme. Does it fulfill its objectives? Do the cinematics reflect the style of the interfaces? How are the screens visually organized? Is there a sense of balance and harmony? What idea or mood do the screens reflect through the use of elements such as cinematics, background colors, and images?

notes

Comp 1

Comp 1

00:00:02:07   00:01:42:21

000067   SHOT124.VER04.EFX002

100%   0;00;02;07   Full   Active Camera

Courtesy of Brian Immel

animatics

objectives

Explore the kinetic experience that is the nature of animatics

Learn the importance of animatics in the studio and usage during on-site shoots

Learn how to time a story for pacing, dialogue, and special effects shots

introduction

Storyboards are a wonderful tool to emphasize character blocking, camera placement, and action, but there are times when storyboards are just not enough to visualize what a shot is going to look like. Animatics became popular to show complex movement and special effects, which are difficult to represent with storyboards. George Lucas was one of the first directors to use animatics for his epic film *Star Wars,* and has used them ever since. By creating animatics, a team is able to grasp whether shot compositions are viable within budget and time constraints. For example, David Fincher created animatics for the action scenes in *Panic Room.* This helped him to gain more control over the images than just working with storyboards. By indicating movement and character blocking within an animatic, he was able to get a feel for how a scene should be shot. More specifically, it allowed Fincher to refine the timing of an action scene, camera placement, and character movement.

This chapter looks specifically at the process for creating animatics in both live-action and animation productions. The chapter also explores several software packages that aid in the creation of storyboards and animatics.

ANIMATICS

WHAT IS AN ANIMATIC?

An animatic is a moving storyboard that helps the director of a production determine how scenes flow together. An animatic begins with the script, which is then translated into storyboards. The individual storyboard panels are then shot with a camera, or scanned into the computer, and edited together in time to a dialogue track. By cutting together live footage, or using a stopwatch to time storyboards, the animatic artist has a guide for how long each movement, dialogue, and action will take. Although these two examples of timing are often used to produce an animatic, the artist should never stick to them religiously. Sometimes the animatic artist may want creative license to emphasize an emotion or an action, in which case the pretimed sequence would not be completely accurate. Nonetheless, without a well-timed animatic, production time for a shot could take three to four times longer to build, causing the studio to lose thousands of dollars and valuable production time.

Who Uses Animatics?

Almost everyone involved in a production can benefit from using an animatic. Animators use the animatic as a template for the scene setup and basic timing. Directors use the animatic to help them visualize scenes. The animatic helps actors who are working with computer-animated characters or objects, to act and react to images that are not there. Special effects artists use the animatic for clearly identifying timing issues. The animatic may also be used in the sound booth to help voice actors get a feel for the action that they are dubbing over. There is no set rule for the number of uses for the animatic. Most studios that use the animatic for preproduction have their own rules governing its uses and functions.

Types of Animatics

There are several different types of animatics that a director may request to help previsualize a shot. The four most common types include hand-drawn animatics, motion tests, videomatics, and 3D animatics.

Hand-Drawn Animatics

Hand-drawn animatics are timed storyboards. The storyboards themselves are hand-drawn sketches that are animated to show how a scene should flow. Such animatics help the director communicate complex action scenes.

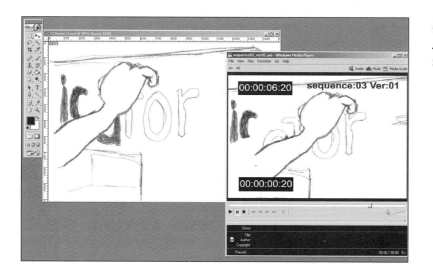

figure | 12-1 |

Storyboard to animatic image.

Pencil Tests and Motion Previews

Pencil tests are commonly found in cel animation. The purpose of a pencil test is to preview the motion of characters or objects. Once pencil tests are analyzed, they are cleaned up by the artist.

figure | 12-2 |

Pencil test/motion preview.

Motion preview, on the other hand, explores various issues including camera movement, character placement, timing, and pacing. For example, George Lucas previewed what a battle sequence of two space ships would look like by cutting together existing WWII camera footage of planes in aerial combat.

Videomatic

A videomatic is a rough videotaped version of a scene that uses actors or production staff to assist in blocking the action, actor placement, timing, and camera angles. Videomatics are usually shot on or near the studio lot, using existing equipment. For example, the director's car might serve as a space vehicle, or a picnic table might be used as a ledge that overlooks a deadly gorge. A member of the production staff usually sits in for an actor, and is shot against a bluescreen.

Bluescreen allows a director to combine two or more pieces of film into one. When an actor is shot in front of a bluescreen, the artist can easily remove the blue background in the computer, and replace it with a matte painting. For example, we have all seen a character dangling from the edge of a building hundreds of feet above the ground. To create such an effect, the actor is shot in front of a bluescreen only a few feet off the ground. The blue background is then removed, and replaced with a new background that makes it appear as if the character is actually sixteen stories high. Usually the directing is minimal and cinematography simple. The idea is to test out the script, timing, and feel of the shot.

The staff will then take the camera footage they shot, and set it up to be automatically captured into the computer. Once the footage is digitized, it is ready for a rough editing session. The staff edits the footage together using low-end, off-the-shelf software. The edited scene is usually finished and ready to be reviewed within a day.

3D Animatics

Some companies opt to make their animatics from computer-generated material rather than hand-drawn storyboards. 3D artists create a low-resolution model (also known as a proxy model) of the set, characters, and props. The 3D artists then animate each shot, applying the basic rules of storyboarding such as blocking movements and camera framing. 3D animatics allow the production team to experiment with different camera positions. Such experimentation is difficult to illustrate in storyboard panels, and cost prohibitive during the actual production.

figure | 12-3

Three camera placements within a 3D animatic.

Rough-Cut Animatics

A rough-cut is a well-developed animatic that is constantly updated with near-completed animation or finished shots. This does not mean the shot is 100 percent complete, but just one step short of being locked. Once a shot is ready for review, the artist replaces the existing animatic shot with the final footage. The updated rough-cut is then presented to the director or department head for approval.

The rough-cut animatic should reflect the tools and techniques needed to create each scene. If a shot requires special effects, the rough-cut should have that same, or approximate, special effect in it. For example, if a live actor picks up a computer generated (CG) object, the rough-cut should show the actor picking up the 3D model, or an approximation of the CG object.

SOFTWARE

Every animatic artist works with software to load the hand-drawn or filmed shots into the computer and manipulate them. There are several storyboard software programs on the market; this book will review several programs that are used to create animatics, including Adobe software programs, Photoshop and After Effects, and software programs developed specifically for creating storyboards.

Adobe Photoshop

Adobe Photoshop is one of the most popular image-editing programs on the market. It allows an artist to produce and manipulate graphics for many mediums, including story-boarding. Using Photoshop, the animatic artist can import sketches, paint storyboard frames, cut out images, create title sequences, and much more.

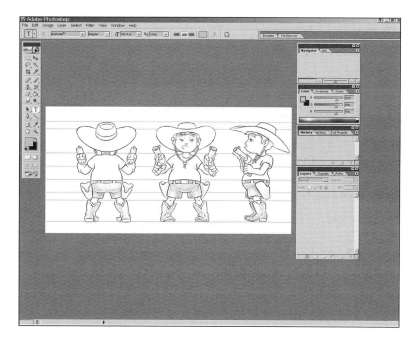

figure | 12-4 |

Photoshop interface.

Adobe After Effects

It is very useful to use nonlinear editing software for creating animatics. One such program is Adobe After Effects. This program allows animatic artists to produce moving storyboards and visual effects. After Effects also creates dynamic camera angles and movement, such as tracking or pan shots. For example, an artist can easily dolly out from a close-up to a medium shot, or boom up the side of a building.

figure 12-5

After Effects interface.

StoryBoard Quick

StoryBoard Quick is a previsualization software program that assists in the creation of production storyboards. The program aids artists and directors with organizing a project and planning shots. The program includes locations, props, and characters in several different positions.

figure 12-6

StoryBoard Quick interface.

FrameForge 3D Studio

FrameForge is a film studio that allows the user to previsualize scripts in a virtual environment. It allows the user to build three-dimensional environments, add props, and block characters in the setup of their shots. FrameForge allows the user to use pan, dolly, and crane shots to capture each shot. The user may also use the software to build shot lists and overhead diagrams.

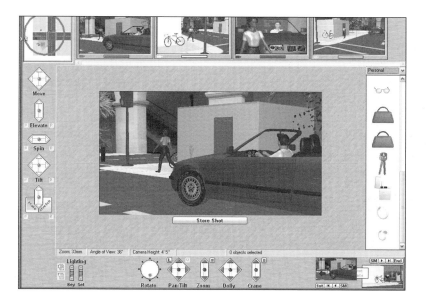

figure | 12-7 |

FrameForge 3D Studio interface.

ShotMaster

ShotMaster provides an environment in which to organize and plan a project. The program also allows creation of shot lists and floor plans, and the use of a preexisting library of characters and environments.

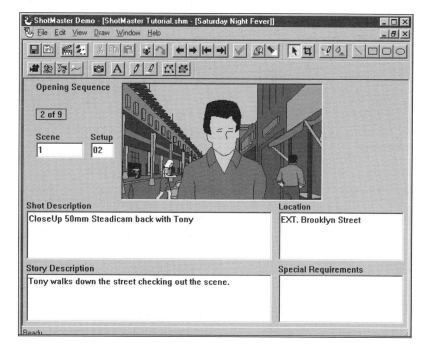

figure | 12-8 |

ShotMaster interface.

SCANNERS

A scanner is a piece of hardware that digitizes images for use in the computer. Each scanner sold today comes with scanning software that works directly with Adobe Photoshop.

figure | 12-9a |

Scanner bed.

Reliable scanning software should allow for contrast and balance adjustments, cropping tools, resolution settings, and color balance. Some scanners come with the capabilities of rotation tools and slide scanning abilities. A good scanner should also be able to scan in both color and grayscale modes, and have the capabilities to do high-resolution scans, which is any resolution above 300 dpi. (*DPI* stands for dots per inch, and always represents a fixed number of dots per linear inch on hardcopy media.)

figure | 12-9a |

Scanner bed.

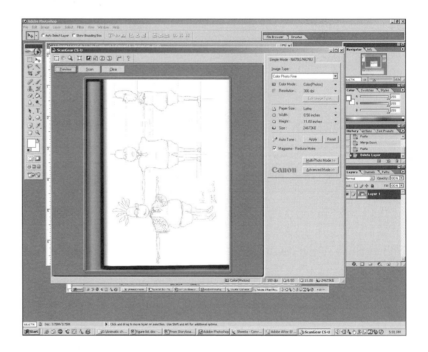

figure | 12-9b |

Scanning software.

Scanning Strategies and Resolution

When scanning storyboards, you need to set the resolution. Television resolution for PCs is 72 dpi at 720 x 480, and Mac, 72 dpi at 640 x 480. Depending on which platform you use—PC or Mac—these will be your choices for the basic composition size of the animatic.

Still Shots and Moving Shots

Basic rule of thumb: always scan larger than you need. Although television resolution is 72 dpi, you never know when the director will ask you to change a still shot to show movement. Having a little foresight could save a few headaches down the road. As a rule of thumb, I scan my images at 150 dpi.

Stills

Still shots should be scanned at 72 dpi, 720 x 480 minimum size, but I always scan at the size of the image, and clean up the resolution later.

Pans

The only consideration you must think about here is the length of a pan. Does the camera pan a full 360 degrees? Can you fit your panning sketch into the scanner?

Zooms

As a rule of thumb, zooms should be scanned at 300 dpi. If you want to be exact, you should figure out how close you are going to get in on the frame. For example, if you are going to move in on the frame twice, scan at twice the base resolution (72 dpi x 2 zooms = 144 dpi).

Saving the Raw Scanned Image

Save the raw scanned images in Photoshop as either TGA or TIFF format. Both of these formats are lossless, which means that the file type does not use any type of compression to store the data within the image. Lossy type files use algorithms to compress the data and with repeated use (opening, saving, closing), the data can be lost over time. Other formats that are lossy are JPEG, GIF, and BMP.

PREPARING STORYBOARDS FOR THE ANIMATIC

It is faster to scan everything all at once, rather than going back and forth between the scanning software and Photoshop. Save each file in Photoshop, and then start cleaning them up for use in programs such as After Effects. It is wise to save the original raw image and work with a copy (File > Save As).

Image Cleanup

Stray lines, dots, fuzzies, and so forth should be removed. Adjust the contrast as needed. Keep white paper white, and the black lines black. Nothing is more distracting than yellowish paper with gray lines that are supposed to represent your storyboards. Most scanning software allows you to adjust the contrast, or you can fix it in Photoshop by adjusting the contrast (Image > Adjustments > Brightness/Contrast) or changing the levels (Image > Adjustments > Levels).

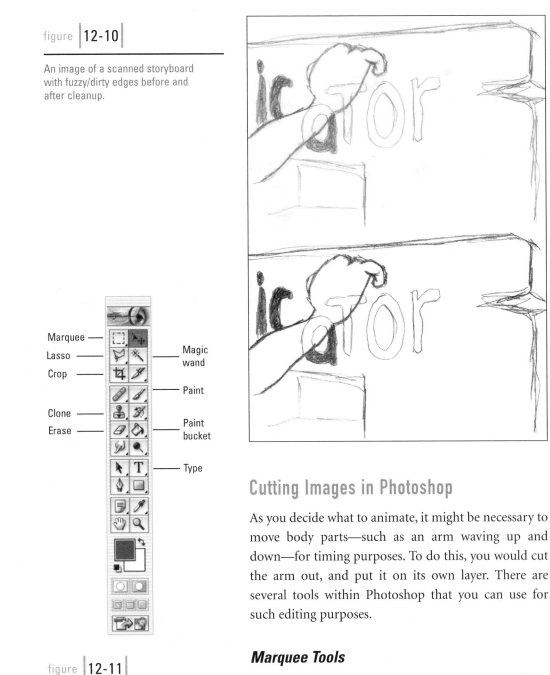

An image of a scanned storyboard with fuzzy/dirty edges before and after cleanup.

Marquee
Lasso
Crop
Magic wand
Paint
Clone
Erase
Paint bucket
Type

figure |12-11|

Photoshop's Toolbox palette.

Cutting Images in Photoshop

As you decide what to animate, it might be necessary to move body parts—such as an arm waving up and down—for timing purposes. To do this, you would cut the arm out, and put it on its own layer. There are several tools within Photoshop that you can use for such editing purposes.

Marquee Tools

The marquee tools are good for selecting large rectangular or elliptical areas.

Magic Wand Tool

The magic wand selects large open areas; it is useful for removing the background color from an image.

Lasso Tools

There are several lasso tools that you can choose from. The lasso acts as a freehand selection tool. The polygonal lasso draws lines to select areas, and the magnetic lasso selects areas based on differences in pixel values. For example, if you have a black-inked line drawing, the magnetic lasso tool will easily pick out the difference between the paper and the lines. If there are shadows, eraser marks, and so forth, then the contrast between pixels will not be as clear, making it harder to pick up with the magnetic lasso tool.

Creating Layers

Organization is extremely important, especially if dozens of layers are imported from Photoshop into After Effects. Therefore, each layer should be named to help keep track of the different images needed for animation purposes.

To Color or Not to Color

Most storyboards are not fully colored, although some elements may be colored to bring attention to particular areas. One example might be a face in a crowd. The face would be tinted a simple color to set it apart from the crowd.

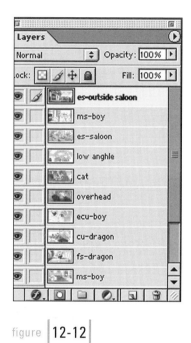

figure | 12-12 |

Photoshop Layers palette.

IMPORTANCE OF TIMING

There are three key elements to keep in mind when considering timing. First, each production has a specified length, whether it is a thirty-second television spot or a two-hour feature film. Second, the mood and pace of a production is determined by the cutting and motion of every scene. And third, acting affects the timing of each shot. Bad timing sticks out like a sore thumb in any medium and any format, whether it is television, film, games, or Web animation.

Development of Timing

Developing good timing in the animatic helps animators with their workload. Frame count, blocking the animation, dialogue tracks, and specific shot movement are the main factors used in determining the timing of the animatic.

Frame counts

Film speed is 24 frames per second (fps), and television speed 29.97 or 30 fps. Knowing the frames-per-second for a project can save you time when creating the animatic. For example, if you have a shot that lasts for two seconds, it will take either 48 frames (film) or 60 frames (TV). This may not seem like such a big difference, but when the shot length increases, you can expect to see disparities. Let's say you have a film shot that lasts two minutes. You will need to animate 2,880 frames at 24 frames per second (2 minutes = 120 seconds, 120 seconds = 2880 frames or 24 x 120). At a television speed of 30 fps, you need to animate 3,600 frames. Now the differences are starting to add up. Consider a two-hour movie!

When creating the animatic, the first thing you will need to decide is how many frames per second. Up until recently, with the advent of CD-ROM games, digital cameras, Web animation, and so forth, all animation was shot on film or 24 fps. Another question you may need to ask is if the animation will be shown in the United States or in Europe. Video (television broadcasts) in the U.S. runs at 29.97 fps. Video in Europe runs at 25 fps. Nowadays with the use of high-grade, high-speed film, some animations are done at 45 to 60 fps. Typically, faster film speeds are used for slow-motion shots or special effects shots. Video games on the average run at 15 fps, but with each new generation of game consoles, the frame rate is getting closer to cinematic levels.

Do We Need That Much Time?

Time is a complicated issue. If a shot is too long, it may slow down the pace and make it boring. On the other hand, if the shot is too short, it may seem ambiguous and confusing. Trial and error perfects our timing skills. If you don't know how long a shot should be, make an educated guess. Remember, the animatic is created to block out timing. Using nonlinear software to edit the animatic makes it easy for animators to add or subtract frames from a shot.

Do I Animate Everything or One Thing at a Time?

Focus on one element at a time. Animating everything at once may seem like a way to save time in a tight production schedule, but more often than not it causes the animatic to have a monotone pace. Keep in mind that you are trying to create a sequence that leads the viewer. When animating frames, you should guide the viewer by drawing attention to where the action is about to happen.

Varying Timing for Expressive Results

So far, we have learned how to give identity to a shot from timing through physical presence. The next step is to use timing to convey emotion and personality. Each emotional state has a distinctive timing associated with it. Take for example a person walking through a house. Depending on the situation, the person may walk cautiously if it is a haunted house, or frantically if trying to get to work on time. Performance is greatly influenced by the mood of the characters and the setting of the shot.

Here are a few thoughts to consider for creating emotion in animatics:

- Sad shots have soft and slow motions.
- Energized shots have fast action and frequent cuts.
- Anxious shots have fast motions, but with long pauses.

Learning How to Time

Some people are naturals at timing, but most of us are not. For those of us who do not have this natural talent, we need plenty of practice. Every animator, whether they are 2D or 3D animatic artists, should own a stopwatch. The hardest part for animatic artist to learn is how to use a stopwatch! This may sound simple, but many animators buy a stopwatch and never use it because they think they already know how long it takes to perform a task. Consider this: How long did it take you to read this paragraph? How long does it take to read it out loud? You will be surprised to see how much time has passed once you start using a stopwatch. With just a few sessions, you should see dramatic improvement in your timing.

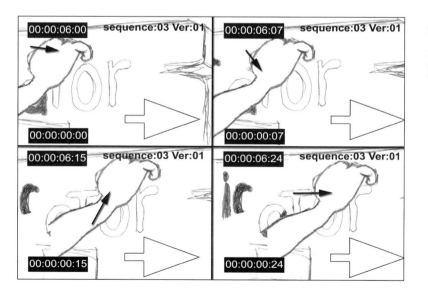

figure **12-13**

Arrow indicates movement in one direction.

Another way to hone your sense of timing is to simply watch others. Watching a movie on a DVD player with frame-by-frame playback can help you determine how long it takes a person to walk across a room, as opposed to a person running away from a mountain lion. Watch to see how other artists have timed out situations similar to your own. Note the differences between the shocked response of a cartoon character to that of a live actor. Another way to learn timing is through observation in the real world. Observe how people interact in public. How long does it take for a child to run around a jungle gym? How about when the child is being chased by a parent or by another child? How long does it take for a person to eat lunch with a group of friends compared to eating alone? After studying how long people take to do their daily activities, compare those times to those found in television programs. What are the major similarities and differences? Does a television program show someone taking an hour lunch, or do they cut it down to the basic components of the lunch break?

Observing everything around you is the first step to learn timing. Break down the motions and timing of people walking, gesturing as they talk, animals running, cars coming to a stop at a light, planes taking off, and so on.

More importantly, use the stopwatch. When you are not sure how long a shot should be, stand up, grab your stopwatch, and time yourself acting out the scene. It may be easier if someone else is running the stopwatch. This way you can concentrate on the actions rather than worrying about stopping it the very moment you are done acting out the scene.

Counting Time

There are two types of stopwatches currently available on the market: analog and digital. Analog watches have a second and minute hand, and are battery operated or hand wound. Digital stopwatches come in a variety of shapes and styles. A good digital stopwatch can record time down to the one thousandth of a second.

Whether you buy an analog or digital stopwatch, make sure it includes a rope to hang around your neck. This may sound trivial, but you would be surprised how many times you will put it down and lose track of the stopwatch.

| TIP |

Watch a cat give itself a bath. Notice how the cat starts at one part of its foreleg and ends at another. Sometimes the cat pauses in between licks to look around. Notice how it wets its foreleg to wash its ears and head. Try to capture those key moments during the bath.

figure | 12-14 |

Analog stopwatch.

figure | 12-15 |

Digital stopwatch.

Do not use any device that does not display seconds or is difficult to handle. Computer clocks typically do not display the seconds or milliseconds. Do not use wristwatches either. Usually the buttons on wristwatches are hard to depress accurately.

What to Animate First

Start with broad, generalized motions first, then work your way down to specific timings. Generalized animation uses the total number of frames it will take to accomplish the motion and timing. Animatics are more or less a collection of generalized animations of the storyboards. By generalized, I am referring to the overall movement and sense of timing within a sequence. For example, a detective walks around the room looking for clues in a wide shot. During his search he may turn over various items, read a page from a diary, and so forth. To animate this sequence, I would have the drawing of the detective wandering around the room like a paper doll cutout with no movement in the legs, arms, or head. The cutout of the detective would pause in each area of the room to allow for the proper amount of time to search there. The right amount of time is dependent on the situation of the shot, and the emotion the animator is trying to express.

DID YOU KNOW

Before the advent of nonlinear editing software, animatics were called leica reels. Leica reels are filmed storyboards that can be projected in synchronization with the soundtrack.

Video Reference

The animator can shoot footage of himself performing the actions, or he can use preexisting footage for timing assistance. You don't have to buy an expensive camcorder to shoot video reference, but it does help. Replicating timing from preexisting footage can be more useful than filming yourself performing the actions. One example would be building a shot of a dog running after a Frisbee (rather difficult to act out yourself, don't you think?). It would be ideal to look for videos that contain the information.

CHAPTER SUMMARY

Animatics are especially important to the production process for complex sequences, special effects, and animation. The animatic begins with storyboards, which are scanned into the computer, and manipulated using software such as Adobe Photoshop and After Effects.

There are numerous types of animatics that a production crew can use, including hand-drawn, 3D animatics, and videomatics.

Hand-drawn animatics are the artist's sketches that are scanned into the computer and timed to a dialogue track. 3D animatics are a bit more sophisticated and include low-resolution models of your characters, objects, and props; these allow the artist to experiment with complex camera moves that would be prohibitively expensive during an actual shoot. Videomatics are a rough videotaped version of a scene that uses production staff to assist in blocking the action, timing, and camera angles.

One of the most crucial elements of the animatic is timing. The animatic artist must time the actions, movements, and dialogue. Identity is given to a scene through timing that shows the personality and emotions of a character. A character that is anxious, for example, has fast motions but with long pauses, whereas a character that is unhappy tends to have soft and slow motions. Timing is learned through practice, and the use of a good stopwatch.

When you begin animating, consider the big picture first. Plan the generalized motions of the characters before you start animating the details, such as arms and legs moving as a character walks. Animate one thing at a time so as not to get confused. As the animatic takes shape, it will help the director visualize ideas, the producers estimate production costs, and the special effects artists estimate timing issues.

in review

1. When are animatics used?

2. What are three types of animatics?

3. Who uses animatics?

4. What is bluescreen?

5. At what resolution should images be scanned for zooms?

6. What does lossless mean?

7. What are several tools you can use to cut images in Photoshop?

8. What are two key elements of timing?

9. What are several ways to hone your timing skills?

10. What is the difference between an analog and a digital watch?

exercises

1. Draw three or four frames from an action movie, scan them, and cut them into animation-ready layers in Photoshop. Time out the action sequence and animate it in After Effects.

2. Using your stopwatch, go to a local park and time how long it takes a person to walk from one location to another. Use a notebook to log the times and put a notation next to the times, describing the mood that person is in. Do this over several days at different hours of the day. You will probably find that every person has a different pace. A woman dressed in a business suit during her lunch hour may be walking faster than a woman pushing a stroller in the late afternoon. Take note of clothing and time of day, and how it affects the timing of the walk.

3. Using at least a dozen or so storyboards of two people talking, create an animatic for a dialogue track. Do not import the sound at first or time the dialogue with a stopwatch. Reading off the script, try to guess how long it takes to complete each shot. After the first animatic is finished, go back and add the dialogue track and see how close you were on the first try.

drawing the human form

objectives

Draw the human figure in proportion

Illustrate quick sketches according to the line of action

Render the human figure in perspective

Draw the human figure in motion

introduction

Most films and animation revolve around the interaction of characters to tell a story.

It is the storyboard artist's job to visually interpret the action of characters from the script; this includes how characters move and how they are framed. For example, an artist may be asked to draw a character about to take the final shot in a tied basketball game. Not only does the artist have to know how to draw the proportions of the basketball player, but he must also capture the tension and movement of that character.

When it comes to materials, each artist has their preference, whether it is using photo-blue pencils or markers. Jack Johnson, illustrator of such films as *Independence Day* and *The Perfect Storm,* for example, sketches out production sets in pencil or charcoal and then paints the final designs in watercolors, oils, or gouache.

This chapter covers the basic techniques for drawing the human form, drawing characters in proportion and perspective, and drawing characters in motion. The chapter also covers materials used for creating storyboards.

figure | 13-1 |

The storyboard artist interprets how characters move within a frame.

Courtesy of Luis Alfaro

Drawing the human form.
© Matt Karol

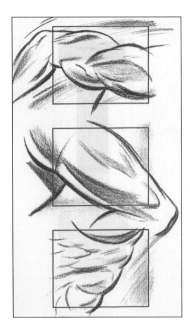

VISUAL REFERENCE

Where do you begin if you have little or no drawing experience, or just need to brush up on your skills? A good place to start is your local library. There are numerous "how to" books, such as *Keys to Drawing* and *Human Anatomy Made Amazingly Easy*, which are devoted to understanding the human figure and how to better illustrate it in your drawings. Another great reference to study is comic books, which have thousands of action poses of characters in all shapes and sizes.

If you have access to a DVD player, you can study movies such as *Monsters, Inc.*, *The Matrix*, and *Terminator 2*, which all contain a supplemental section on storyboards. There are also illustration books that highlight storyboarding art, including *Final Fantasy: The Spirits Within*, *The Art of Mulan*, *The Matrix*, and *Gladiator*.

SIMPLIFYING THE HUMAN FORM

Remember those stick figures that you used to draw as a kid? Sometimes the head was too big or the arms were too long. Sometimes you may have dressed the figure in a skirt or a pair of pants. Drawing stick figures is not all that uncommon when creating roughs or thumbnail storyboards. In fact, many directors draw out their ideas using stick figures before the work gets assigned to the storyboard artist.

When drawing thumbnails or roughs, you may choose to begin with the stick figure because of its simplicity. Drawing stick figures allows you to compose a frame quickly before moving on to more complicated forms. They are also useful for drawing within a smaller space, like the storyboard frame, allowing you to draw figures of any size confidently before adding detail.

| TIP |

Start a scrapbook of images from fashion and sports magazines, comics, photos, and anything else you might find of interest.

figure | 13-3 |

Thumbnail drawings.

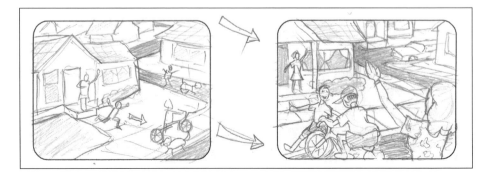

GESTURE DRAWING

Action, movement, attitude, and rhythm: these are qualities that you should convey in your drawings. It doesn't matter if you studied fine art, or cartooning, as long as you can express the action of a figure.

Observing characters in real life will assist you in creating realistic drawings. That is why it is always a good idea to carry a sketchbook with you. Don't worry about creating complete drawings. It is more important to get the gesture down, which is the first step toward drawing figures.

| TIP |

Just like practicing music scales, gesture sketching can be used as a warm-up exercise. You may warm up by drawing fast circles, ovals, and lines before beginning your drawings.

figure | 13-4 |

Quick gesture drawings.

When starting a figure drawing, you should always begin with the line of action, which is an imaginary line that extends through the main action of a figure.

Gesture lines are drawn quickly and freely to establish the mood and movement of the figure. The line of action helps accentuate the overall flow of a pose, and should be drawn in one stroke, keeping it loose rather than stiff and formal.

If you look at a skater, for example, you would follow the curve of the body from the head down to the leg that holds the skater's weight. For the skater, there would be two lines of action—one that runs through the body and one that goes through the arms. By adding the second line through the arms, the fluidity of the pose is increased, making it more pleasing to the eye.

figure | **13-5**

Follow the curve of the skater's body.

Gesture drawings are extremely helpful to the storyboard artist, whose ultimate goal is to render dozens, if not hundreds, of panels in a short period of time. J. Todd Anderson, for example, rendered over 600 rough pencil sketches in a matter of six weeks for *Fargo*. Artists for the animated series *The Simpsons* render over 800 in a two- to three-week period. To reach these levels, you must practice every day for several hours a day. The goal is not to create a great piece of art, but rather to get ideas down in a quick and cost-effective way.

THE HUMAN FIGURE IN PROPORTION

When drawing the human figure, many artists commonly use the head as a measuring tool. This is extremely helpful when first learning figure proportion.

The average human figure, from the top of the head down to the bottom of the feet, is about eight heads tall, although an action hero may average nine heads.

figure |13-6|

Practice drawings of the human figure in proportion.

Let's take a look at the average human figure that is eight heads high:

- The distance from the head to the top of the chest is about two heads.

- The distance from the chest to the top of the thighs is about two heads.

- The distance from the top of the thighs to the knee is about two heads.

- The distance from the knees to the feet is about two heads.

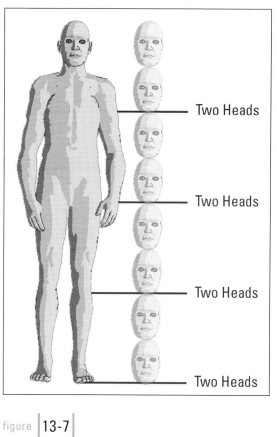

Two Heads

Two Heads

Two Heads

Two Heads

figure |13-7|

Average height is between 7 1/2 and 8 heads high.

The Head

What is the first thing you notice about a person? Is it the eyes? Perhaps it is the smile. When we look at someone, we do not necessarily notice the shape of someone's head. As an artist, you must look beyond the aesthetics to learn the basic techniques for drawing a well-proportioned head.

Some of the most common problems when drawing facial features include eyes that are too close together, a mouth that is adjacent to the chin, and noses that are either extremely long or short. There are numerous techniques to create well-proportioned facial features. One technique is to draw three horizontal lines within the construction of the head. These horizontal lines represent the eyes, mouth, and nose. You can create a triangle from the eye line to the mouth line. The triangle is a useful facial diagram that will assist you in arranging features in an aesthetically pleasing manner.

As a storyboard artist, you will need to draw the human head in many positions. For example, if a character's head is tipped forward, facial features will gather toward the chin. When tipped backwards, facial features move toward the forehead.

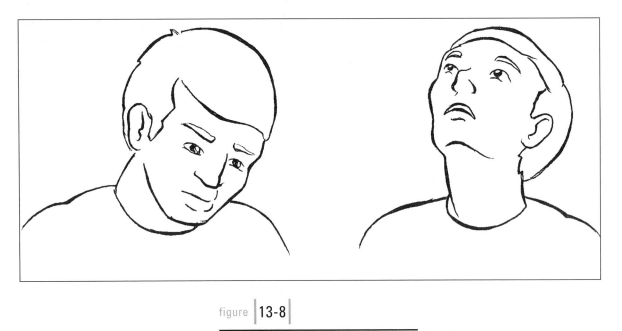

figure | 13-8 |

The human head tipped forward and back.

Hands

Hands are one of the hardest parts of the body to draw accurately. In animation, many artists create a simplified hand having only three fingers and a thumb, which is much easier to draw. Mickey Mouse and Bart Simpson, for example, have only four fingers.

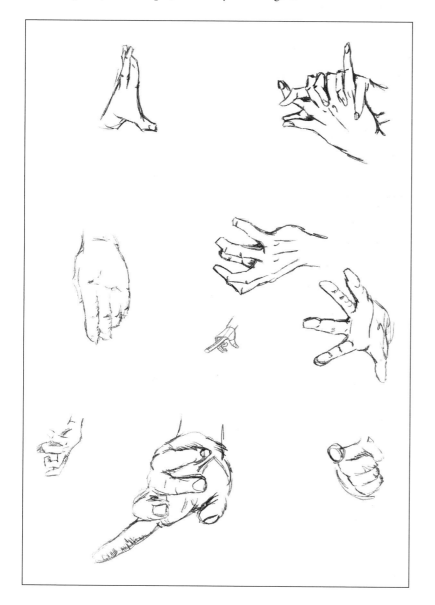

figure | 13-9 |

Hands in various positions.

| TIP |

Use your own hand as a model when drawing the hand in various positions. It also helps to draw the hand and fingers as cube forms with the shape of the fingertips as slightly triangular.

There are three main parts of the hand: the fingers, palm, and thumb. The palm of the hand is somewhat thicker near the wrist and is larger on the thumb side.

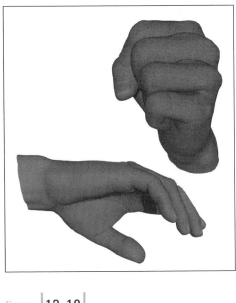

figure | 13-10 |

Three parts of the hand: fingers, palm, and thumb.

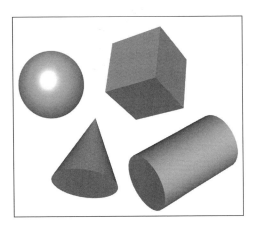

figure | 13-11 |

Geometric shapes.

figure | 13-12 |

Artist mannequin.

There will be many occasions as a storyboard artist when you will need to draw the hand in numerous positions: clenched fist, gripping hands, a hand holding a glass, and so forth.

GEOMETRIC SHAPES

The human figure is three-dimensional; therefore, your drawings should reflect the volume and weight of the human figure. After drawing gesture lines, you can simplify the figure into a few basic shapes, including spheres, cylinders, and cubes. These shapes not only make it easier to draw a character, but geometric forms add the illusion of depth to the two-dimensional surface of drawing paper.

An arm, for example, is made up of cylinders. The fingers are made up of cubes. By applying solid shapes to the figure, you can establish the height, width, and three-dimensional roundness to a character.

As a storyboard artist, you should always be looking for ways to break down an object, or person, into geometric shapes. Using an artist mannequin is an extremely useful tool since its three-dimensional shape is made up of cylinders and spheres. Joints are moveable so that the mannequin may be positioned in a variety of movements. Once you are able to draw the proper shapes, the details should come easily.

figure | 13-13 |

Begin with the line of action.

THE FIGURE IN MOTION

You want your storyboards to show the action and attitude of a figure. For example, pay attention to how a woman walks. Does she stride gracefully? Is her walk determined? How does she hold her head? The more knowledge you have of how a person moves, the easier it will become to render figures in motion.

Begin your action poses with the action line, which assists in placing the various parts of the figure in the proper position, before adding detail.

Many directors require storyboard artists to draw the figure in action. If a figure is walking, for example, you want to start shifting the weight from one foot to the other side of the body in your figure drawing. Alternately, as the right leg swings forward, the right arm swings back. The longer a stride a figure makes, the more pronounced the arms swing. The motion of a runner follows the same principles, but the movement is much more pronounced. The body is thrust forward, and the motion of the body is exaggerated.

figure | 13-14 |

Figure in motion.
Courtesy of Matt Karol

figure | 13-15 |

Rule of threes.

| TIP |

Remember the rule of threes when sketching the human figure: the chest, waist, and hip; upper arms, lower arm, and hand; upper leg, lower leg, and foot.

THE HUMAN FIGURE IN PERSPECTIVE

One of the fundamental challenges facing the storyboard artist is to represent three-dimensional figures on a flat two-dimensional surface. As discussed in Chapter 6, there are a number of techniques to establish depth. The technique covered in this chapter is called size perspective, which refers to the apparent reduction in size of an object as it moves into the distance. To illustrate size perspective, you must first understand how the horizon line and the vanishing point contribute to the illusion of depth. The horizon line is an imaginary line that is always at eye level, and vanishing point is when two lines converge at some distant point on the horizon.

Taking these two concepts into consideration, distant figures will appear smaller, but have the same shape and proportion as they would close up. Now, characters standing together are the same height; this is our point of reference. But if character *B* dashes toward us, about fifty feet away from character *A*, he will appear larger, and so on.

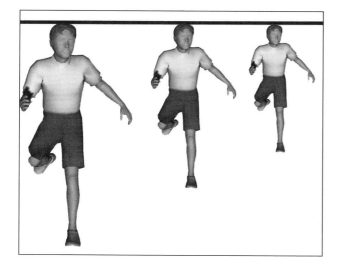

figure **13-16**

Three runners in perspective.

Applying perspective to your figures will also assist you in creating dynamic camera angles and depth of field. For example, an overhead shot of a person in perspective will appear diminished compared to a character drawn from a low angle.

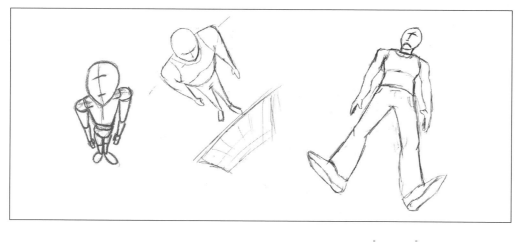

figure **13-17**

High- and low-angle drawings of characters.

WRAPPING IT UP

Characters come in all shapes and sizes, therefore, as a storyboard artist you should be able to draw many different types of figures—from an old woman to a 16th-century warrior. It is important not just how they look, but how they move or stand, and their relative size compared to their environment. Another consideration is clothing. You should have a basic knowledge of fabric and how it pulls or compresses. This is especially noticeable at the joints, such as the elbows, wrist, and knees. For example, fabric usually gathers up at the waistline, which causes tightly compressed folds.

The most important thing to remember when drawing clothing is the figure beneath the fabric. Clothing should reveal the figure's shape first, before moving into the detail of dress.

MEDIA AIDS

When drawing storyboards, you should become familiar with the materials available for rendering illustrations. This is especially important when working under tight deadlines because many materials take time to master.

For easy reference, I've divided my recommendations for materials into three categories: presentation materials, drawing aids, and drawing accessories. This is not an exhaustive list, but more of a starting point. If you are new to the storyboarding process, begin with materials you are familiar and comfortable with. As your storyboarding experience grows, experiment with a wider variety of materials.

Presentation Materials

Storyboard layouts range from one panel per page to the popular format of six to nine panels per page. Action, audio, and special effects are noted below each frame, as necessary. Storyboard templates offer artists a ready-made format to work from. You may buy storyboard templates at an art store or you may create your own. One advantage of store bought templates is that perforated lines separate each frame, making it easy to detach individual frames if the story sequence needs to be changed or frames deleted.

You may prefer to draw your own storyboard panels, either out of personal preference or to suit specific client requirements. They are best created on standard 8 1/2 x 11-inch bond paper, which makes for easier photocopying and faxing. The simplest way to create storyboard panels is on a computer, but they can also be drawn with a pen and ruler.

figure | 13-18 |

Storyboard templates.

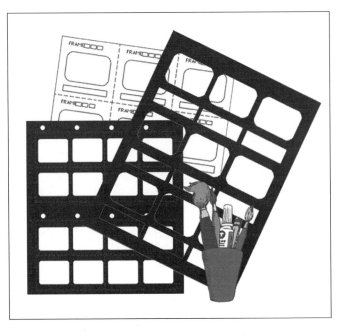

Storyboards produced for commercial presentations are mounted on heavy-weight black card stock. Storyboard mats that you buy commercially are die-cut templates that allow you to trace one storyboard panel at a time.

Drawing Aids

For the storyboard artist, drawing aids may range from the simple graphite pencil to the more elaborate setup of using charcoal or paints for presentation storyboards and concept illustrations.

Pencils

The pencil is the storyboard artist's basic tool. Most storyboard artists begin sketching in pencil because of its erasability. Many artists create their underdrawings using a nonphoto blue pencil, which is virtually invisible when photocopied, or a 2H graphite pencil, which produces light lines.

Graphite pencils vary in degrees of hardness; softer leads (B series) deliver darker lines, whereas hard leads (H series) render light, thin lines. The B series range in hardness from B (hardest) to 8B (softest). The H category ranges from H (softest) to 9H (hardest). The most common pencils used by storyboard artists are the B, HB, and 2B pencils, which are of average hardness, and the 4B, which is soft and dark and works well for quick sketches. These pencils are preferable for faxing and photocopying because photocopier machines more easily read their thicker lines.

figure | **13-19** |

Graphite pencils.

Mechanical pencils are also an option. Many artists prefer mechanical pencils simply because they don't need to be sharpened. Mechanical pencil lead is sold loose and comes in the same degrees of hardness as graphite pencil lead.

Charcoal

Charcoal is a great tool and the most widely used medium, after the graphite pencil. Charcoal is available in three types: compressed, charcoal pencil, and vine. Compressed charcoal comes in stick form and produces strong blacks and bold lines. Charcoal pencils, which look similar to graphite pencils, are versatile and are the best choice for small-format works that require fine lines. Vine charcoal (sticks) is the least permanent form. This type of charcoal produces very soft effects and works well for quick gesture drawings.

figure 13-20

Charcoal pencils.

Colored Pencils

Colored pencils are thick and waxy, and come in varying degrees of hardness. The most popular brand on the market is Prismacolor, which is made by Sanford Company. These pencils are soft and allow for heavy application of color. Another popular brand of colored pencils is Prismacolor Verithin, also made by Sanford. These pencils are harder than the Prismacolor pencils, and produce crisp lines.

figure 13-21

Colored pencils.

Colored pencils are best used for creating slight changes in color gradation. For example, colored pencils can realistically create the reflection of the moon illuminated on water or the subtlety of a person's skin tone by simply applying the right amount of pressure and blending. Colored pencils can also be used on top of colored markers to create subtle highlights or shadows.

Markers

Markers are the tools of choice in the advertising world. They deliver the "flash" that most advertising campaigns require. Markers are inexpensive, dry quickly, and come in a variety of colors and tip shapes.

There are dozens of ink colors and shades to choose from, including fluorescent and metallic colors. The most popular among artists are gray markers, which come in a full range of shades from 10 percent to 100 percent. Gray markers are very useful when illustrating objects in black and white and when adding depth to objects. Warm grays have more of a brownish tint. Cool grays have a slightly blue tint.

figure | 13-22 |

Markers.

Tip shapes have a direct result on line thickness. Broad tips are best used to cover large areas of an illustration, such as the body of an airplane, the sky, or a truck. Fine-tipped markers are great for smaller areas and detail work, such as rendering fabric detail or wood grain.

I suggest using marker paper when using markers. The paper has a medium absorption rate, which makes for crisp lines and intense colors. Marker paper comes in 9 x 12-inch, 14 x 17-inch, 11 x 14-inch, and 19 x 14-inch sheets, so if storyboards need to be distributed to crew and coworkers, they must be scaled down to standard 8 1/2 x 11-inch size.

Pens

There are many different types of pens on the market, but the most popular among storyboard artists is the technical fountain pen. Most storyboard artists like technical pens because they handle just like a pencil and come in a wide variety of point sizes, from very fine to very broad.

Technical pens deliver fine lines of consistent width; therefore, they work extremely well for drawing within smaller formats like the storyboard frame. Technical pens are an ideal choice for lettering. They are also useful for adding texture and detail to drawings.

Most storyboard artists will create their underdrawing in pencil, then do the finished drawing right on top, using a technical or ballpoint pen. The reason is that ink is extremely unforgiving; you cannot cover it with heavier lines or erase it.

figure | 13-23

Technical pens.

Gouache

Gouache is a very useful tool among production illustrators who render film sets before they are constructed or illustrators of highly detailed presentation storyboards.

However, it is not the type of aid that an artist would use for production storyboards because gouache is an opaque watercolor that is used primarily to add highlights to artwork. For example, gouache would be an excellent choice for depicting mist from a waterfall or a rain-slicked street.

figure | 13-24 |

Gouache.

Drawing Accessories

When drawing a complex figure, such as a spacecraft, building, or automobile, you should use tools that produce these shapes more accurately than drawing them freehand. A few templates that assist in the creation of backgrounds such as trees, mountains, and crowds, include the triangle, French curve, and straight edge ruler.

The kneaded eraser and hard eraser are also essential materials when you create storyboards. The kneaded eraser is pliable and is best used for light erasures; the hard eraser is used for eliminating denser lines.

Masking tape is an effective method for controlling marker placement, and is best used when the area to be colored is straight. If curves need to be drawn, they must be cut out of the masking tape with an X-Acto knife before being placed on the drawing. Alternatives to masking tape are friskets, which are transparent sheets of acetate with an adhesive on one side. Similar to masking tape, shapes can be cut out with an X-Acto knife, then placed on the drawing.

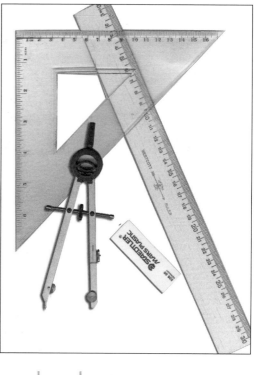

figure | 13-25 |

Drawing accessories.

CHAPTER SUMMARY

When beginning your figure drawings, there are a few simple techniques that you should follow. You should start by creating a visual library that includes magazines, photographs, comics, and other materials that you may find useful. As a storyboard artist, you will most likely be required to draw many panels per day. Therefore, it is vital to practice your gesture drawings every day for several hours a day. When you draw your figures, start with the line of action, which will accentuate the overall flow of a pose. Once you understand human proportions, block in your figure with solid shapes.

There is a plethora of drawing aids available to the storyboard artist, including pencils, charcoal, colored pencils, pens, and markers. The pencil is the artist's most basic tool, which ranges from soft leads (B series) to harder leads (H series). Markers are used predominately for presentation storyboards, and come in a variety of colors; technical pens come in a selection of point sizes, from very fine to very broad.

in review

1. Why do many artists begin by drawing the stick figure?

2. What are gesture drawings? Why are they used as warm-up exercises?

3. Why are gesture drawings important to the storyboard artist?

4. How is the average human figure measured?

5. What is one of the hardest parts of the body to draw?

6. Arms are made up of what type of shape?

7. What is the main purpose of the storyboard artist when drawing figures?

8. Why is applying perspective so important when drawing the human form?

9. What is the storyboard artist's most basic tool?

10. Graphite pencils vary in degrees of hardness. What pencil is best for faxing and photocopying?

11. Broad-tipped markers are good for rendering what type of scenes?

exercises

1. Gesture drawings are done within a short period of time. In this exercise, you will draw thirty gestures. Set a kitchen timer. Start your gestures at three minutes, working your way down to thirty seconds for a human figure. If possible, use a live model; otherwise, use a mannequin that you can pick up in any art store.

2. Pick a shot from a movie. Now pause your DVD. Sketch what you see within the frame. You have one minute. After each minute is up, choose a new shot to sketch within a one-minute duration.

3. Pick your favorite animated character. Sketch the character in various poses. You have one minute. After each minute, draw a new pose.

the business of storyboarding

objectives

Understand the criteria needed to create an online portfolio versus a flat-art portfolio

Explore techniques for interviewing for a job

Explore the skills needed for acquiring a storyboard position

introduction

How do you land your first storyboard gig? Ask ten different artists how they got their first job, and they will each have their own unique story to tell. However, there are steps that every artist can take to enhance their marketability. This chapter explores several strategies for getting your first job, including volunteering on student projects, internships, and networking. This chapter also covers the state of the industry, how to sharpen your storyboard skills, and how to create both flat-art and online portfolios.

THE BUSINESS OF STORYBOARDING

INDUSTRY

The first step for any potential storyboard artist is to research the industries and clients that use storyboards.

As a storyboard artist, it is your job to familiarize yourself with the nuances of the various industries that hire storyboard artists. You may begin your research by studying industry magazines. Your local library will most likely have a variety of magazines covering the film, animation, advertising, and gaming industries.

The following is a list of magazines that cover the business of animation and film:

'boards

This magazine covers the business of commercial production. Some of its features include notable work by the top advertising agencies, highlights from animation and FX companies, audio and postproduction, and the director's chair.

Animation Magazine

Features the art of animation, including industry interviews, festivals and events, jobs, and visual and EFX.

FilmMaker

Covers independent filmmaking and filmmakers, offering an array of information on independent productions, tips, and resources.

MovieMaker

MovieMaker includes interviews with some of the top actors, directors, writers, and cinematographers. The magazine also includes notices for jobs.

American Cinematographer

Explores cinematography tips and techniques, reviews, and interviews with some of the top cinematographers.

When you begin your research, you should focus on what projects are being produced, budgets, and their need for illustrators or storyboard artists.

SKILLS

A normal workday for a storyboard artist might include drawing between twenty and thirty finished panels. If deadlines are not met, chances are the artist will not be hired again. Therefore, several hours a day should be dedicated to practicing technique and speed. A common technique I use in my own class is to have students study live-action and animated movies. Students survey several scenes to understand the visual storytelling process. They are then required to storyboard between twenty to thirty shots from a scene and critique them in terms of shot composition, movement, proper camera terms, screen direction, and mood. Storyboarding action sequences is extremely useful because many live-action films are rich in visuals and complex movement. Other techniques to improve drawing skills are to take life-drawing classes and practice your gesture drawings.

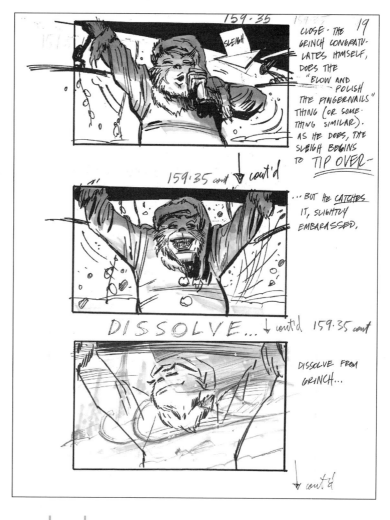

figure **14-1**

Storyboard from *How the Grinch Stole Christmas*.
Courtesy of Universal Studios

PORTFOLIOS

The main purpose of a portfolio is to show it to potential employers. But how do you make it stand out from other artists who are also submitting their work? As you start to sort through your storyboard samples and put your portfolio together, you should always keep in mind your audience. Knowing who your audience is will help you to set your goals and organize what goes into a portfolio. Portfolios should be customized for each interview.

figure | 14-2 |

Animation storyboard.
Courtesy of Steven Hok

A portfolio is your opportunity to shine. You should include only your best work, which shows off your creative skills and your ability to communicate complex story ideas. It is always wise to have action sequences in your portfolio that highlight dynamic framing and compositions. Include different types of projects to show your range as an artist and a storyteller. Use samples from different product categories. Also, think about including self-driven projects, from concept sketches to final illustrations for a product. You want to show potential employers that you can solve problems, especially when it comes to complex sequences.

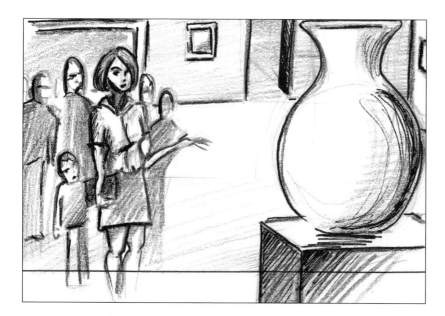

figure | 14-3 |

Rough sketch that exaggerates foreground elements.

Courtesy of Jamie McCullough

Online Portfolios or Drop-Off?

There are many art directors who require artists to drop off their portfolios before granting an interview. When submitting artwork, it is recommended that you **never** submit originals. Rather, you should send high-quality duplicates of your work to potential employers. If no work is available at the time of submission, many employers will keep your work on-file for future jobs. Therefore, when sending duplicates make sure your portfolio is a convenient size so that it may be easily filed in storage. A recommended size is 8 1/2 x 11 inches.

Checklist for Storyboard Portfolio

- Each storyboard sequence should be self-explanatory
- Submission should be 15-20 samples
- Place best work first and last
- Action Scene
- Character Designs
- Backgrounds
- Gesture Drawings
- Rough Sketches
- Group work according to subject and content

Online portfolios are extremely popular these days, especially amongst freelance storyboard artists. Digital portfolios are a great resource for potential employers to get a first impression of an artist's work.

figure | 14-4 |

Model sheet.
Courtesy of J. Allen McFadden

As in your flat-art portfolio, when developing samples for your digital portfolio, always keep in mind your target audience. Also, get feedback on the content and design of your portfolio before you upload it to the Internet. The initial building of the content and images may take a bit of time, but once you have it uploaded, it is much easier and cheaper to update than flat art. There are portfolio sites accessible by employers, where artists can submit their work. Therefore, it is advisable to research online companies that promote storyboard artists.

Portfolio Organization

There are many ways to organize a portfolio that best fits your personality.

Chronological

Chronological is a system where you organize material by date. Put your most recent work first, since it is probably your better work.

Category

Divide your portfolio into sections. You can categorize many different ways, including by different types of pieces (roughs, animation 'boards, and concept illustrations).

Complexity

You can group work according to project. For example, an advertising job includes thumbnails, roughs, and final storyboards.

STRATEGY FOR GETTING YOUR FIRST JOB

How do you get your first storyboard job if no one will hire you without "real-world" experience? This is a reasonable question that constantly comes up with students who are considering careers as storyboard and concept artists. Even if you have created a stellar portfolio, you will still need to be proactive in seeking opportunities that will enhance your hireability. Potential opportunities include student projects, internships, and networking.

Student Projects

You might consider volunteering on student films. The number of film schools and video departments around the country is currently on the rise. Contact local colleges and university film departments in your area and inquire about current and upcoming projects. There is usually a dedicated space where you can put up flyers advertising your skills. Consider storyboarding student shorts in exchange for a film credit.

Internships

Getting an internship is a great way to get your foot in the door. Sometimes an internship leads to a job if you show yourself to be talented. Several businesses to explore include gaming companies, theme parks, local advertising agencies, Web design studios, and, of course, animation and film studios. Internships can be acquired through university career centers, word of mouth, and professional advertising and illustrator organizations.

Networking

Networking is a process that includes developing a list of contacts that will help you to uncover job opportunities. The first step is to contact the people that you do know. They may have words of advice for you, or they may know other individuals who could potentially help you. Once you have exhausted your own list, the next step is to contact people that you do not know. The best place to start is local workshops and associations. Join organizations for illustration, film, video, and multimedia. Industry organizations are wonderful opportunities to meet people who work in your field. You should also contact local production companies. Every city has a production book that lists individuals who work in video and film for that area. One book is the *Motion Picture, Film and Theater Directory*, which is a portable directory that lists film and video facilities. You can order this directory and others online. Contact people on the list who may be able to help you, and have your name placed on this published list.

figure | 14-5 |

Extended storyboard frame of a tilt up.
Courtesy of Thomas Mahoney

DO I NEED AN AGENT?

You should consider acquiring an agent when you have a well-crafted portfolio and a few professional credits to your name. Once you have a stellar portfolio, start sending it out to agents. Most agencies that handle storyboard artists are located in Los Angeles. You will need to have a short, yet comprehensive and well-written query letter to send along with samples of your work.

The agent acts as the middleman for you. Once you hire an agent, he should handle the details of booking jobs and contract negotiations. This is especially helpful to the artists who do not want to be continually looking for jobs. The agent will pay you directly, instead of the advertising agency or studio. He will usually take a 15-25 percent cut from your pay for his efforts.

Agent Checklist

- How long has he been in business?
- What are some of the jobs he has gotten for clients?
- How does he plan to "sell" you to clients?
- Ask if you can contact several of his references.
- How fast will you get paid once a job is complete?

Having an agent is not necessary, but it can be helpful in getting your name out there. Make sure when contacting agents that you do your homework. Have a list of questions prepared to ask agents regarding the process for sending you on jobs, and how you will get paid. Remember, you are interviewing them as well, and when it comes to your career, you are the one in charge.

THE COVETED JOB INTERVIEW

You landed your first interview. Now what?

First, do your homework. Learn everything you can about the company and potential job. If you are meeting with a game studio, for example, I suggest you research the key players, the mission and the culture of the studio, and the style of the game products. Also, prior to the interview, ask for a written job description. This will often contain details not included in the original job posting.

The next step is to practice. Come up with a list of potential questions the interviewer could ask you. Go over your answers several times. If you can rehearse with someone who is experienced in the job interviewing process, do it. The more prepared you are, the more confidence you will exude.

Potential Questions to Ask an Interviewer

- On a typical day in this position, what would I do?
- What training is required for this job?
- What abilities are important to being successful in this job?
- What is the most satisfying part of the job? Most challenging?
- How did you get your job?
- What opportunities for advancement are there in this field?
- What entry-level jobs are best for learning as much as possible?
- Is there a demand for people in this occupation?
- What advice would you give a person entering this field?
- If you could do things all over again, would you choose the same path? Why?

You practiced your interviewing skills, researched the company, and have clean copies of your resume and business cards on hand. You also have what you think is an exemplary portfolio, tailored specifically to that job. None of that will matter if you do not arrive on time. Get specific directions and leave early enough to arrive on time for the interview. If you are early, walk around the block or find a quiet place where you can think about your questions.

Be positive. You never want to walk into an interview and appear desperate for the job. Just as you were proactive in your job search, the interview requires self-initiative as well. Ask questions. While presenting yourself as someone eager to get to work, also present yourself as someone looking for the right job fit. Remember, you are interviewing them as well.

Be enthusiastic. Remember, you are selling yourself. If you are not passionate about your talent, you cannot expect someone else to be interested. Speak enthusiastically about your experiences and skills.

Follow up with a thank-you letter. This is an absolute must.

This list is just an overview. The more interviews you get, the better prepared you will be when the right one comes along. Even if you are not interested in a job, go on the interview anyway. You never know where it may lead.

Resources on the Internet

There are a plethora of resources on the Internet specifically targeted to the job search. Topics include:

- Targeting and Researching Employers
- Executing Your Job Search Campaign
- Interviewing and Negotiating

CHAPTER SUMMARY

You have the skills and talent to become a storyboard artist, now comes the hard part—finding work. As a storyboard artist, you need to familiarize yourself with the market; what studios are producing projects that have a need for storyboard artists.

To land that first gig, you need a stellar portfolio to show to potential employees. As you put your portfolio together, keep in mind your target audience. Portfolios should be customized to the job you are interviewing for. Your portfolio should include your best work, including action sequences, concept sketches, and figure drawings.

Landing the first job is always the hardest. Several ways to increase your chances include internships, working on student projects, and networking. Once you have acquired the interview, you need to prepare. Research the studio you are interviewing with, and practice your answers to potential questions.

in review

1. What materials should go into your portfolio?

2. Why is it important to network?

3. What is the role of the talent agent?

4. What are several strategies to assist with landing the first job?

5. What is the average workday for a storyboard artist?

exercises

1. Research an animation, film, or game studio. Find out everything you can about the company, including:

   • History of the company

   • Benefits

   • Corporate structure

   • Advancement opportunities

2. Research online agencies. Find out everything you can, including their:

   • Client roster

   • Fee

   • Placement percentage

appendix A

The following illustrations are storyboard templates based on television and film aspect ratios.

1.33 aspect ratio

Scene _____   Shot ____

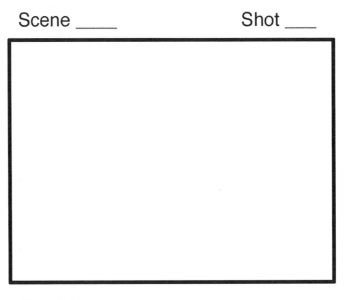

Description: _____

_____

_____

1.85 aspect ratio

Scene _____   Shot ___

Description: _____

_____

_____

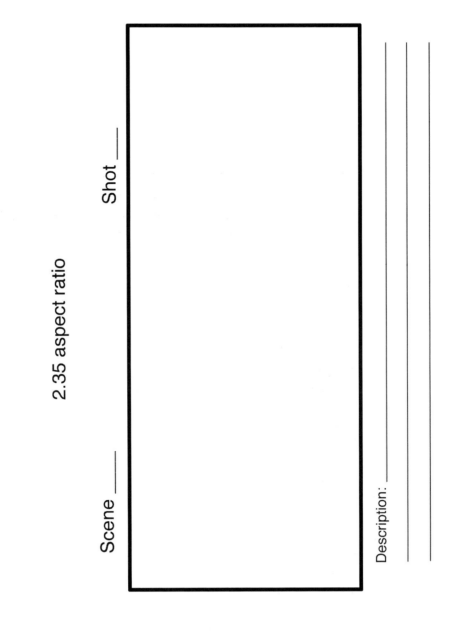

2.35 aspect ratio

Scene _____

Shot _____

Description: _____

appendix B

BOOKS

Today there are many books that illustrate the art that goes into the making of feature animation and live-action films, along with useful reference books on filmmaking and screenwriting. The following lists include some very good reference books for art, animation, film, screenwriting, and special effects.

Art Books

The Making of Star Wars
by Laurent Bouzereau

Art of the Empire Strikes Back
by Valerie Hoffman

The Art of Star Wars, Episode II: Attack of the Clones
by Mark Cotta Vaz

The Art of Finding Nemo
by Mark Cotta Vaz

The Art of The Return of the King (The Lord of the Rings)
by Gary Russell (Author), Peter Jackson

The Art of The Two Towers (The Lord of the Rings)
by Gary Russell

The Art of the Matrix
by Spencer Lamm

Exploring the Matrix: Visions of the Cyber Present
by Karen Haber (Editor)

The Art of Monsters, Inc.
by Pete Docter (Introduction), John Lasseter (Introduction)

Gladiator: The Making of the Ridley Scott Epic
by Ridley Scott (Introduction)

Tim Burton's Nightmare Before Christmas
by Frank Thompson

Planet of the Apes: Reimagined by Tim Burton
by Diana Landau (Editor), et al

Terminator 2: Judgment Day: The Book of the Film
by James Cameron and William Wisher

The Making of Final Fantasy: The Spirits Within
by Steven L. Kent

Future Noir: The Making of Blade Runner
by Paul M. Sammon

*Film Architecture: From Metropolis to
Blade Runner*
by Dietrich Neumann

Batman & Robin: The Making of the Movie
by Michael Singer

Inside Men in Black II
by Brad Munson

Visions of Armageddon
by Mark Cotta Vaz

*Paper Dreams: The Art & Artists of Disney
Storyboards*
by John Canemaker

*Wallace & Gromit–"The Wrong Trousers":
Storyboard Collection*
by Brian Sibley

*Walt Disney's Nine Old Men & the Art of
Animation*
by John Canemaker

Dinosaur: The Evolution of an Animated Feature
by Jeff Kurtti

Animation

*How to Draw Animation: Learn the Art of
Animation from Character Design to
Storyboards and Layouts*
by Christopher Hart

*The Animation Book: A Complete Guide to
Animated Filmmaking–From Flip-Books to Sound
Cartoons to 3-D Animation*
by John Canemaker (Introduction), Kit Laybourne

*The Animator's Survival Kit: A Manual of Methods,
Principles, and Formulas for Classical, Computer,
Games, Stop Motion, and Internet Animators*
by Richard Williams

Acting for Animators
by Ed Hooks

Timing for Animation
by Harold Whitaker, John Halas

Animation: From Script to Screen
by Shamus Culhane

The Illusion of Life: Disney Animation
by Frank Thomas and Ollie Johnston

Producing Independent 2D Character Animation
by Mark Simon

Stop Motion: Craft Skills for Model Animation
by Susannah Shaw

Film

*The Visual Story: Seeing the Structure of Film,
TV, and New Media*
by Bruce Block

Understanding Movies
by Louis Giannetti

Directing: Film Techniques and Aesthetics
by Michael Rabiger

*Film Directing Shot by Shot: Visualizing from
Concept to Screen*
by Steven D. Katz

*Setting Up Your Shots: Great Camera Moves
Every Filmmaker Should Know*
by Jeremy Vineyard, Jose Cruz

*Film Directing, Cinematic Motion: A Workshop
for Staging Scenes*
by Steven D. Katz

The Art of Watching Films
by Joseph M. Boggs, Dennis W. Petrie

*The Film Director's Intuition: Script Analysis and
Rehearsal Techniques*
by Judith Weston

Digital Cinematography & Directing
by Dan Ablan

*The Complete Guide to American Film Schools
and Cinema and Television Courses*
by Ernest Pintoff

*Masters of Light: Conversations with
Contemporary Cinematographers*
by Dennis Schaefer and Larry Salvato

Digital Lighting & Rendering
by Jeremy Birn

Picture Composition for Film and Television
by Peter Ward

Myth and the Movies: Discovering the Mythic Structure of 50 Unforgettable Films
by Stuart Voytilla, Christopher Vogler

Special Effects

Industrial Light & Magic: The Art of Special Effects
by Thomas G. Smith

Film Tricks: Special Effects in the Movies
by Harold Schecter

Men, Makeup, and Monsters: Hollywood's Masters of Illusion and FX
by Anthony Timpone

Special Effects: The History and Technique
by Richard Rickitt

Screenplays

Screenplay: The Foundations of Screenwriting; A Step-by-Step Guide from Concept to Finished Script
by Syd Field

Teaching Scriptwriting, Screenplays, and Storyboards for Film and TV Production
by Mark Readman

From Script to Screen: The Collaborative Art of Filmmaking
by Linda Seger, Edward Jay Whetmore

Story: Substance, Structure, Style, and the Principles of Screenwriting
by Robert McKee

The Writer's Journey: Mythic Structure for Writers
by Christopher Vogler

Making a Good Script Great
by Linda Seger

Drawing

The New Drawing on the Right Side of the Brain
by Betty Edwards

Keys to Drawing
by Bert Dodson

The Artist's Complete Guide to Figure Drawing: A Contemporary Perspective on the Classical Tradition
by Anthony Ryder

Drawing Realistic Textures in Pencil
by J. D. Hillberry

Drawing the Head & Figure
by Jack Hamm

Secrets to Drawing Realistic Faces
by Carrie Stuart Parks

Master Class in Figure Drawing
by Robert Beverly Hale, Terence Coyle

Drawing People: How to Portray the Clothed Figure
by Barbara Bradley

Perspective Made Easy
by Ernest R. Norling

Draw 3-D: A Step-by-Step Guide to Perspective Drawing
by Doug DuBosque

Perspective for Interior Designers
by John Pile

Dynamic Figure Drawing
by Burne Hogarth

Drawing Cutting Edge Comics
by Christopher Hart

Drawing Dynamic Hands
by Burne Hogarth

Advertising

Ogilvy on Advertising
by David Ogilvy

Campaign Strategies and Message Design: A Practitioner's Guide from Start to Finish
by Mary Anne Moffitt

appendix C

A list of DVDs featuring storyboards.

2 Fast 2 Furious (2003)

A.I. Artificial Intelligence (2001)

Amelie (2001)

American Beauty (1999)

Armageddon (1998)

A Beautiful Mind (2002)

A Bug's Life (Collector's Edition) (1998)

Alien: Special Edition (1979)

Baby Boy (2001)

Babylon 5: In the Beginning (1993)

Back to the Future: Trilogy

Beauty and the Beast (1991)

Brazil (1985)

Cape Fear (1991)

Cast Away (2000)

Cats & Dogs (2001)

Citizen Kane (1941)

Clerks: Uncensored—The Animated Series (2000)

Contact (1997)

Dante's Peak: Criterion Collection (1997)

Deep Blue Sea (2000)

Die Another Day (2002)

Die Hard (1988)

Edward Scissorhands (1991)

Fight Club (1999)

Futurama

Ghostbusters (1984)

Gladiator (2001)

Godzilla (1998)

Hollow Man (2000)

Independence Day (1996)

Jaws (1975)

Jurassic Park: The Lost World (1997)

King of the Hill

Matrix Revolutions (2003)

Men in Black (1997)

Minority Report (2002)

Monsters, Inc. (2001)

Moulin Rouge! (2001)

Planet of the Apes (2001)

Psycho (1960)

Pulp Fiction (1993)

Rebecca: Criterion Collection (1940)

Se7en (1995)

Shrek (2001)

Signs (2002)

Snatch (2000)

Snow White and the Seven Dwarves (1938)

Spartacus (1960)

Spider-Man (2002)

Spirited Away (2001)

Star Trek II: The Wrath of Khan (1982)

Superman (1978)

Tarzan (1999)

Terminator 2 (1991)

The Abyss (1989)

The Beach (1999)

The Exorcist (1973)

The Fast and the Furious (2001)

The Godfather: DVD Collection (2001)

The Lord of the Rings (2001)

The Matrix (1999)

The Mummy: Ultimate Edition (1999)

The Nightmare Before Christmas (1993)

The Patriot (1999)

The Prince of Egypt (1998)

The Rock (1996)

The Silence of the Lambs (1991)

The Simpsons: The Complete First
Season (1989/1990)

The Sixth Sense (1999)

Titan A.E. (2000)

Total Recall (1990)

Tron (1982)

Twister (1996)

Vampire Hunter D: Bloodlust (2000)

Walt Disney Treasures: Silly Symphonies
(1931-1939)

Who Framed Roger Rabbit? (1988)

William Shakespeare's Romeo + Juliet (1996)

index